Reviews for *Requiem for a Lawnmower*

"Extremely well-written. I'm going to tell everyone I know about it."
—Ken Druse, gardening author

"*Requiem* gives the back-to-nature gardening movement a much-needed boost of literary experience and love of place that has been painfully absent."
—*Wildflower Magazine*

"The tone is as comfortable as a porch swing." —*Dallas Morning News*

"Want to see the last of the noisy, gas-guzzling, time-and-energy consuming lawnmower? Read Sally and Andy Wasowski's informative and fun-filled *Requiem for a Lawnmower.*" —Memphis Horticultural Society

"Down home, common sense, and sometimes brutally honest perceptions. Some will make you laugh, and all will make you think." —*Fine Gardening*

"No less than a watershed work that has signaled the native plant movement's coming of age." —Louisiana Native Plant Society

"It's humorous, it's chatty, it's full of useful information." —*Florida Gardener Magazine*

"A fun, fresh perspective." —*Carolina Gardener Magazine*

"A delightful adventure into gardening." —*Gardens Magazine*

"Carved-in-stone gardening ideas could be changed forever. . . . This book is common sense, logical, and right as rain!" —*Organic Digest*

"*Requiem* is one of the most charming and useful volumes I've seen lately."
—Judyth Rigler, Southwest Bookshelf

"This book reads well. It's fun and serious at the same time. And the essays are potent." —Fort Worth *Star-Telegram*

T0066565

"It's not easy to espouse native plants without sounding preachy, but it's been done and done well by the Wasowskis." —Betsy Jukofsky, Hilton Head Packet

"*Requiem* is a delightful adventure into this new-wave gardening. The Wasowskis's wit and wisdom shine through." —*Gardens & More Magazine*

"Finding *Requiem* was like finding a superhighway with all the right signs after going every which way for a worrisome time." —*Brandon News* (Florida)

"The Wasowskis write in a very personal, informal style that is easy and enjoyable to read." —Oklahoma Native Plant Society.

"*Requiem* is more of a sit-down-and-enjoy book that'll delight you with wit as well as wisdom. The Wasowskis are dedicated to making gardening more pleasure than toil." —*Houston Chronicle*

Requiem for
a Lawnmower

Other books by Sally and Andy Wasowski

Native Texas Plants: Landscaping Region by Region

Native Texas Gardens: Maximum Beauty, Minimum Upkeep

Gardening with Native Plants of the South

Native Landscaping from El Paso to L.A.

The Landscaping Revolution: Garden with Mother Nature, Not against Her

Building Inside Nature's Envelope: How New Construction and Land Preservation Can Work Together

Gardening with Prairie Plants

Requiem for a Lawnmower

Gardening in a Warmer, Drier World

Second Edition

Sally Wasowski
and Andy Wasowski

Cartoons by Vahan Shirvanian

TAYLOR TRADE PUBLISHING
Lanham • New York • Dallas • Boulder • Toronto • Oxford

Copyright © 2004 by Sally and Andy Wasowski
First Taylor Trade Publishing edition 2004

This Taylor Trade Publishing paperback edition of *Requiem for a Lawnmower*
is an original publication. It is published by arrangement with the author.

All rights reserved.
No part of this book may be reproduced in any form or by any electronic or
mechanical means, including information storage and retrieval systems, without
written permission from the publisher, except by a reviewer who may quote
passages in a review.

Published by Taylor Trade Publishing
An imprint of The Rowman & Littlefield Publishing Group, Inc.
4501 Forbes Boulevard, Suite 200
Lanham, Maryland 20706

Distributed by National Book Network

Library of Congress Cataloging-in-Publication Data

Wasowski, Sally, 1946–
    Requiem for a lawnmower : gardening in a warmer, drier world /
Sally Wasowski and Andy Wasowski ; cartoons by Vahan Shirvanian.
— Sec. ed.
        p. cm.
    Includes bibliographical references and index.
    ISBN 1-58979-063-4 (pbk. : alk. paper)
    1. Native plant gardening—United States. 2. Landscape gardening—
United States. I. Wasowski, Andy, 1939– II. Title.
SB439.W38 2004
635.9'5173—dc22   2003024509

♾ ™ The paper used in this publication meets the minimum requirements
of American National Standard for Information Sciences—Permanence of
Paper for Printed Library Materials, ANSI/NISO Z39.48–1992.
Manufactured in the United States of America.

Dedicated to our mothers, Sara and Sophie

Contents

Foreword

~

When Andy and I first wrote *Requiem for a Lawnmower* in 1991, I thought of native plants as the tough ones, plants that survived on rainfall alone and needed a bare minimum of TLC. In my own garden, once it was mature, I watered just two or three times a year—mainly to keep it looking its best. I weeded and pruned, but still had to give plants away to find room to try something else. I had seen native plants die in the wild only, it seemed, because of human activities: bulldozers, chainsaws, deliberate poisonings, arson, imported insects and diseases, or simple mismanagement.

I worried that our remaining prairies, forests, and seashores would fall prey to farmers, lumberjacks, and development, but I thought that native plants themselves would be able to survive. I no longer think so.

Today, I see native plants dying because of climate change. In north central New Mexico, acres and acres of pines are dying. The cause is listed as beetles or fungus, but the real cause is drought and higher-than-normal temperatures. If the drought lasts even two more years, which is very likely, parts of Santa Fe and Los Alamos will no longer be covered with ponderosa pine forests and pinyon-juniper forests. They will more closely resemble juniper grassland—a habitat that was previously farther south and at a lower elevation, butting right up to desert grasslands. When an entire ecosystem changes, the animals that depend on it die. Many birds and mammals in the southwest get their main sustenance from pine nuts.

I can hear you thinking: Won't the pines come back when the drought ends? Possibly. Tree rings show that the last 800 years have seen regular droughts as severe as the present one. But global warming may be making a difference. In the drought of the 1950s, pinyons died on the south-facing

xi

slopes of the Rio Grande gorge, and they didn't come back, even with intervening wet years.

Climate change is normal; nature is not static. It is possible that our earth would be warming on its own, but I am persuaded by the evidence I've seen that human activities, if they haven't caused this global warming, have at least exacerbated it. Drought-stressed native plants from Texas to California, often the oaks and pines that are the cornerstones of whole ecosystems, are dying in frightening numbers.

In the past, cool-loving plants adapted to a warming climate by migrating toward the poles or to higher, more temperate elevations. This time around, freeways and interstates, cities and suburbs, and thousands of square miles of farmland prevent plants and animals from migrating.

Besides global warming, we as a nation are still losing prairies (now only remnants are left), forests, rivers, and topsoil to human activities such as development, logging, mining, pipelines, and farming.

It's true that there are more nursery-grown native plants for sale today and there is more public awareness of environmental issues. But we, the treehuggers of America, have not yet persuaded our politicians and fellow citizens to change the direction in which we are headed. Even though our lives and futures depend on the health of the environment, protecting the environment still ranks relatively low in polls reflecting voter concerns.

We can help by establishing wildlife corridors and restoring waterways. As private citizens we can vote, donate money to environmental causes, and show up with shovels to accomplish such tasks. But another way we can help is to make the land we own, however small, a haven for native plants and animals.

Our hope is that this book will help educate you, inspire you, and send you into the garden—and the voting booth—with a fresh perspective.

Sally Wasowski
Taos, New Mexico
August 2003

Introduction to the Second Edition

∽

Andy

A lot has happened since Sally wrote the introduction to the first edition of *Requiem for a Lawnmower* well over a decade ago. For one thing, many environmental problems that were serious then are more so today. Overpopulation, greenhouse warming, the disappearing ozone layer, endangered plant and animal species . . . the list is depressingly long. And not the least of these woes is our global water crisis.

In 1993, soon after *Requiem* first came out, *National Geographic* published a Special Edition titled *Water: The Power, Promise and Turmoil of North America's Fresh Water*, edited by William Graves. In his Introduction, Graves stated that "The problem is not the *supply* of water; earth has virtually the same amount today as it did when dinosaurs roamed the planet. The problem," Graves wrote, "is simply people—our increasing numbers and our flagrant abuse of one of our most precious, and limited, resources."

More than a decade later, things are worse than ever. In March of 2003, the *Washington Post* reported on a 600-page study, issued by the United Nations, on the world's limited reserves of clean, fresh water. This study, called "the most comprehensive assessment of the planet's most essential natural resource," predicted that as many as 7 billion people in sixty countries could face water scarcity by the year 2050. Commenting on this study, Koichiro Matsuura, director general of the UN's Educational, Scientific and Cultural Organization, stated that, "Of all the social and natural crises we humans face, the water crisis is the one that lies at the heart of our survival and that of our planet Earth."

This echoes a warning given the previous year by Maude Barlow, one of Canada's leading spokespersons on biotechnology, when she said, "We cannot overstate the crisis of the world's fresh water situation. Worldwide, the consumption of water is doubling every twenty years. That's twice the rate of the increase in human population. By the year 2025," she says, "our demand for fresh water will exceed nature's ability to supply it by 56 percent."

Most people are either unaware of this, or they're told by certain radio pundits that it's a blatant exaggeration. Well, suppose it is. Maybe we'll only exceed the supply by 20 percent. Or 10 percent. Gee, I was starting to get worried there!

The media report on droughts, of course; pretty hard to ignore when a large part of the country is getting half the annual rainfall it's supposed to get. Or less. And they report when communities issue restrictions on washing cars and watering lawns. But how often do you see a story telling us that maybe having a water-guzzling lawn isn't such a great idea? That maybe we can conserve a lot of water by simply changing the way we landscape our homes and businesses? How much water? Consider this: There are somewhere close to 40 million acres of lawn in the United States. That's 50 million lawns around our homes, plus 700,000 athletic fields, 14,500 golf courses, and thousands of corporate landscapes. Now consider that American homeowners pour approximately 50 percent of their household water on their lawn-centered landscapes. That's over 270 billion gallons every single day—enough water to let every person in the world take a shower four times!

Sally and I live in northern New Mexico. Beautiful country. Clean air. Gorgeous forests. Spectacular mountains. Paradise, yes? Pretty much. But we're an arid state. Annual rainfall is somewhere around six to twenty inches a year, depending on which part of the state you're talking about. In the northern part of the state, where we live, snowmelt factors into the equation. That's when things are "normal." But lately, we've been really dry. We're getting less than half the rainfall we're supposed to be getting. Our last few winters have seen a few snowfalls, but also daytime temperatures in the forties, so what snow we do get melts away pretty quickly and doesn't accumulate enough to saturate the ground in spring. And, a few weeks ago, one of the Tiwa shamans at the Taos Pueblo predicted this wasn't going to change for at least five more years. Some NASA scientists say the figure is more like ten to fifteen years!

Those gorgeous forests are dry and we've already had numerous fires in the state. And recently our local newspaper ran a story on how the water table in our marshy pastureland in El Prado has dropped from less than one foot to eight feet. In an adjacent area, the water table dropped from five feet to twenty-five feet. The grasses are still dormant from last winter, and now it's September. Are we concerned? Oh yeah! Big time! The water table affects the aquifers, and the aquifers supply our wells. Sally and I get our water from a well.

Would we be better off living somewhere else? You tell me. Are you experiencing warmer, drier weather where you live? Chances are, yes. Two years ago I spent three weeks on a speaking tour of the Deep South, where they get lots more rain than we get. But everywhere I went in Alabama, Mississippi and Louisiana, folks told me they were twenty to thirty inches below their normal rainfall. At this writing, nothing has changed. In Mendocino, California, where we go every year for our ocean-fix, and where they too rely on wells, people were telling us the water situation is dicey. And last July I saw a story on CNN reporting on how low New York State reservoirs were that summer.

Since *Requiem for a Lawnmower* came out in 1992, Sally and I have done five more books, traveled to every state in the United States except Hawaii, and talked to hundreds of people: other garden writers, landscape architects and designers, nursery owners, water department employees, and average homeowners. And one thing became clear: virtually everyone was concerned that things are getting worse, not better.

So, when we had the opportunity to bring this book out as an updated, expanded second edition, the first thing we did (after telling the publisher, yes!) was to change the subtitle to *Gardening in a Warmer, Drier World*. Sally and I are strong believers that, now more than ever, native plants and a more naturalistic approach to landscaping are the wave of the future. We call it common-sense landscaping—working *with* Mother Nature, not fighting her.

The original edition emphasized native gardening as a low-maintenance, easy-on-the-back approach to home landscaping. That's still a very attractive benefit for many people. This new edition attempts to focus a little more sharply on the use of native plants as the environmental alternative to traditional landscaping. Readers who recall the first edition will notice that we've added five new chapters and revised many of the original chapters with new information and insights that we didn't have a decade ago.

Will native landscaping solve all our environmental problems? Of course not. But going on as we've been doing for the past one hundred and fifty years will only exacerbate the situation. We've tried to make this book as readable and accessible as possible, because we want you to enjoy your time in these pages. But more, we hope you'll agree with us and join us in spreading the word.

Talk to the media and insist that they cover the solutions and not just the problems. Closer to home, make sure your neighbors know you don't appreciate the toxic chemicals they spray on their yards (and let drift into yours). Organize a neighborhood movement to eliminate or at least dramatically reduce thirsty lawns. Stand against your town's unjust weed ordinances. Join the native plant or wildflower society in your area. Support area nurseries that grow and sell native plants, as well as well adapted, non-invasive exotics.

In short, join us and become a botanical missionary. And wear the label proudly.

Andy Wasowski
Taos, New Mexico
September 2003

Introduction to the First Edition

~

Sally

Most people go through their entire lives without a single epiphany. I've had two.

The first one happened on September 27, 1980, and I have my Aunt Martha to thank for it. She called me up one day and told me about a gardening seminar she'd heard about.

"You'd probably enjoy it," she said. "It has to do with gardening with those wildflowers you're so crazy about."

In fact, as it turned out, that seminar dealt with far more than wildflowers; it introduced me to a whole new category of plants: natives! I heard for the first time the startling news that one could landscape with a wide repertoire of natives: not just wildflowers, but shade trees, ornamental trees, groundcovers, shrubs, vines . . . as well as perennials and annuals in staggering varieties. This was—and still is—a fairly radical notion for traditional gardeners, which I readily admit to being in those long ago days.

That seminar presented an impressive array of speakers, all of whom had grown, collected, and selected native plants with a horticultural eye. Two speakers in particular—Carroll Abbott and Benny J. Simpson—were *so* inspiring that they literally changed the direction of my life.

From then on, whenever and wherever they spoke in the area, I was there—just like a jazz fan going to hear Ella, or a Trekkie off to meet

Leonard Nimoy. When I heard that both were going to be guest lectur-
ers at a landscaping course at Texas Woman's University, I got permission to leave work early every Friday so I could drive to Denton to take
their classes.

I should point out that I was not professionally involved in landscaping at that time; I was a social worker. But I'd always had a love affair with
gardening. Some of my fondest memories are of my Grandmother Hudson
leading me by the hand around her garden. And, no matter where I've
lived—Texas, New York, Virginia, Illinois—I'd always had a flower garden,
composed primarily of plants that I'd scrounged out of alleys or vacant
lots. These were, of course, native and some naturalized flowers, although
I didn't even know those terms then. Yet I think I knew instinctively that
these hardy blooms would do well for me. You see, the truth is, despite my
love of flowers, I'm simply not willing to devote the many hours it takes
to keep more finicky flora looking their best.

Until that seminar, my interest in gardening had been very casual and
largely unfocused. Certainly, I had never considered making it a career. I
was a plant collector, rather than a designer, and I strolled around in my
garden the way I still visit museums, taking in just one thing at a time. And,
even though I'd had art training in college, it had never occurred to me
that I might actually design a landscape of my own, let alone for clients
who would pay me real money for my ideas.

Those gardens that I'd had back then were already established when I
moved in; I had just puttered with them a bit, trying something here,
something else there. Once, while living in Corning, New York, I added
dozens of feet of flower beds to the existing plot. But they were all in
straight, narrow lines around the perimeter of the lawn. This was how my
grandmother had done it; it wasn't very creative or aesthetically rewarding, but it sure made weeding easier. As I said, traditional.

I've always considered a garden an outside room, a place to sit in and
watch the sun go down, or to have a picnic in, or a nook to lounge and read,
surrounded by sweet scents and the hum of bees. I certainly never considered a garden as a place to put in a lot of hard work, watering and weeding
and deadheading. And, especially, mowing! In other words, what I'd always
dreamed of was a garden that required as little effort as possible.

Until that seminar, that's all it was, a dream. But suddenly, here were
these people telling me that what I'd been looking for all my life was possible. I really could have plants that virtually took care of themselves, *beautiful* plants that didn't demand that I devote all of my spare time to their
welfare. Using native plants, I quickly realized, meant that gardening was

no longer dependent on how far the garden hose could reach or how big a water bill one was willing to endure.

As I said, my life changed directions. I began to learn all that I could about these marvelous native plants. And Benny Simpson, a kind and generous gentleman who is now gone, became my mentor, guru, and treasured friend.

Eventually, I found the nerve to actually try my hand at a few landscape designs for people other than myself, first for family members and then—miracle of miracles—for a few brave souls who were actually willing to pay to be guinea pigs. I didn't charge them very much at first because my work wasn't worth very much. In fact, I thought I might be downright dangerous.

Old ideas die hard. Looking back, I now realize that I made many mistakes because I still thought in traditional terms; almost all of the unsuccessful plants I put in were from standard-issue nursery stock. Of course, those same mistakes were being made every day by "real" professionals. They still are! And those native plants that I was experimenting with turned out to be my triumphs.

As for that second epiphany—well, that happened over lunch about five years later. Dayton Reuter, a professor at the University of Texas at Arlington and a talented landscape architect, had seen my first book, *Landscaping with Native Texas Plants,* a book Andy and I wrote for the simple reason that I needed such a resource in my landscaping business and none existed. My landscape plans in that book represented pretty innovative ideas for the time—a woods in the front yard, a bird garden, and a patio garden with no lawn—but I was still thinking of native plants as substitutes for standard gardening fare.

Dayton had been trained in the traditions of that Midwestern genius Jens Jensen, who in the early decades of the twentieth century started using native plants to re-create prairie and woodland habitats.

With the gentle tact found in truly gifted teachers, Dayton made me realize how rigid my thinking still was, and he taught me to think of plants not just as individuals, but as integral parts of a plant community. Moreover, for these plants to succeed as a community, they must all be native, or indigenous, to the same site, such as your property, and not merely native to a political unit, such as the state you live in.

It was as if he'd flipped on the light switch in a dimly lit room. Suddenly I understood that I was free to toss aside traditional thinking and create truly natural landscapes, real woods and prairies and meadows, where all the plants are indigenous and arranged so that they relate to each other as they do in nature. After all, these natives had evolved together, so they already know how to grow together in harmony. A whole new world of design ideas had been opened up for me.

People often ask me about my qualifications for doing landscape design. I patiently explain that, no, I am not a landscape architect, that is, a degreed professional who deals primarily with the construction aspects or hardscaping of landscaping. Surprisingly, very little of a landscape architect's training is devoted to plant materials. And, of that, almost none deals with native plants. Dayton Reuter, and a handful of other LAs I've met, are the exceptions, not the rule.

Landscape designers—at least the ones I know—are, first and foremost, plant people. They are artists who often come from a variety of backgrounds. It is not unusual for a landscape designer and a landscape architect to combine their skills on projects; I've worked that way many times.

I have found that my lack of formal training in either landscape design or standard horticulture has, for the most part, been an asset. Because I was free of the dogmas with which, I feel, many university-trained professionals get saddled, I was able to grasp Dayton's ideas without feeling like a heretic. Without any formal schooling in landscaping, I was able to examine *all* of the possibilities; I wasn't hampered by preconceived notions of right and wrong.

Because of my second epiphany with Dayton Reuter, I began observing entire plant communities and re-creating them in semicivilized forms in the gardens I designed.

The more I observed, the more I realized that plant communities were habitats, and that plants, animals, soil, water, and rocks all logically and naturally fit together. This led inescapably to a closer look at what is happening to our land, our water supplies, and our ecology. And I came to believe that watering, fertilizing, poisoning, and other ways in which we manipulate nature are extravagances that will not be options for us in the future.

I'm convinced that we need to completely change our whole approach to gardening. We need to look at the basics again and see how Mother Nature, the best gardener of all, has managed these many millennia. The more I learn about her, the more she fascinates, teaches, and inspires me.

Frequently, Andy and I are asked to give talks about native plants. It's exciting to address a crowd of several hundred native plant enthusiasts.

But, whenever we do, we have to remind ourselves that, outside that auditorium, there are countless thousands of people in that town who don't have any idea what native plants are, and why it is so vitally important that we use them around our homes and, yes, businesses, as well.

We hope that if you are one of the unconverted, you will read this book and enjoy it. And who knows? Maybe the experience will trigger an epiphany for you, too.

Sally Wasowski
Dallas, Texas
December 1991

PART I

Going Back to Basics

Let a man drink or default, cheat on his taxes
or cheat on his wife, and the community
will find forgiveness in its heart. But let
him fail to keep his front lawn mowed,
and those hearts will turn to stone.

—WILLIAM ZINSSER,
Electronic Coup de Grass: The Mowing Ethic

"Get out the leaf blower, George!"

~

Stop Fighting Mother Nature

~

Sally

Ever wonder why there are so many weekend gardening shows on the air all over the country? Why major retail chains—Sears, Home Depot, Wal-Mart—devote a large portion of their floor space to gardening centers? And why the gardening section of your bookstore is as crowded as the shelves devoted to cookbooks and wonder diets?

The implication seems to be that gardening is an incredibly tough undertaking. Not only do we need an army of experts to advise and guide us, but we also must put forth Herculean efforts, pruning, weeding, watering, and mowing if we want our landscapes to survive and look pretty. And we have to spend tons of money at our neighborhood nurseries and garden supply centers for seeds, chemical fertilizers and insecticides, and replacement plants for the last bunch we bought that seemed to die at an alarming rate.

Conventional gardening—the type practiced by the vast majority of American homeowners—calls for just this sort of all-out effort. And the reason is simple: *To a great degree, we are fighting Mother Nature. We are doing it the hard way.*

Dear reader, we have good news for you. It doesn't have to be that way!

Believe it or not, your garden can look terrific all year with minimum upkeep and watering, and no toxic chemicals at all. All you have to do is start relying on those wonderful native plants that Mother Nature put in your area thousands and thousands of years ago. That's what makes a plant a native: it has been around for so long that it has learned how to cope with the unique conditions in your area.

Do you live in a part of the country that gets just a few begrudging inches of rain each year? The local native plants do just fine with picayune amounts of water that would kill your average nursery flora. And, if you live in coastal wetlands, with annual downpours that seem to encourage ark-building, be assured that the native plants that evolved in your region are quite happy with all of that moisture.

Do you live on acid soil? The native plants in your area thrive in it. Do you have surprise spring freezes? You can't fool the local native plants; they've learned how to wait out the weather; they start blooming when the warm weather has come to stay.

Landscaping with native plants is just plain common sense.

So, you may well ask, why did it take so long—not until the 1970s—for us to start waking up to this fact? Why have native plants taken a backseat to imported varieties for as long as we Americans have been gardening for pleasure? Let's take a quick history lesson:

When European settlers came to this land centuries ago, they had their hands full just surviving. They had to cope with harsh weather, swamp fever, and ongoing conflicts with indigenous people who, for some obscure reason, weren't terribly thrilled about being pushed off their land by these palefaced strangers. Whatever gardening these settlers were doing was limited to coaxing a few crops out of the ground so they could eat, or to growing the medicinal herbs they were familiar with.

Eventually, of course, life got easier for them. Three square meals a day became pretty standard, and our forebears looked around one day and realized that their hardscrabble frontier existence was becoming pretty civilized.

Now it was possible for them to garden for pleasure and for aesthetic reasons, not just to put a bowl of beans on the dinner table. Naturally these settlers wanted their new gardens to *look* civilized. And where were the most civilized gardens they knew? Why, back home, of course—Northern Europe, where they or their parents had come from.

So, they imported seeds and saplings from the Old World and planted their new gardens with flowers and shrubs that had evolved in Europe and the Middle East: horse chestnut, English boxwood, lilac, roses (eglantine, French, cabbage, Damask, and dog), and flowers such as clove pink and sweet pea. Some plants did well and some did not, and some have lived for centuries in watered gardens, but have died in neglected ones.

Europeans were colonizing the rest of the world and explorers were sending back horticultural treasures from the remote lands of their empires. Thus, as time passed, the plants being imported to the Americas via Europe included new and exciting discoveries from Africa, India, Australia, and Japan.

As for all of the colorful and hearty native American flowers, trees, shrubs, vines, and groundcovers that were thriving all about—right under the very noses of the settlers—well, these were considered "weeds," hardly fit company for those cultivated imports. The exceptions were a few natives such as flowering dogwood and Virginia creeper that had been shipped off to European gardens as the strange and wondrous offerings from the North American part of the British Empire. In England— or France or Germany—American natives were cultivated, hybridized, and shipped right back again—but now possessing the glamour of European civilization.

In all fairness, it's hard to blame those settlers for their snobbish attitude toward the native plants. The natives, you see, were growing wild and uncared for. Some of the trees had unpruned dead wood, the result of droughts and ice storms. While some of the native shrubs were browsed and shapely, others were plain scraggly. And how could you value something that grew everywhere for free and that grew so well that you didn't have to work to have it?

Interestingly, it didn't occur to anyone that their beloved imports were also natives—albeit to other parts of the world. The difference was, they'd had the benefit of proper breeding and selection, and were given coddling in the garden. A high percentage of the imported plants you buy today at your local nursery are graduates of this selection process and come from test beds in Europe and Japan.

It wasn't until the mid- to late 1970s that a remarkable thing began to happen. Gardeners started noticing the thousands of native plant species all over the country. Why this change of attitude? In a word, water. We were looking at increased salinity and pollution and droughts and, thanks to our soaring population, greater demands on our finite supply of water. People began to look on the native plant movement as, potentially, the most significant occurrence in the history of gardening since the invention of the garden hose. The garden hose meant, of course, that an entire landscape became dependent on irrigation. With water rationing, drought-tolerant plants suddenly looked more interesting. And native plants began a steady rise in popularity.

Today, virtually every state has an active native plant and/or wildflower society. National and regional gardening magazines regularly feature articles on natives. Botanic gardens and arboretums all over the country are displaying native plants and are even recreating native plant habitats. Master Gardeners are trained in techniques of how to conserve water and coached in the beauties of their local native plants. Even garden clubs, long-time bastions of traditional gardening, now include programs and speakers on natives, and many have added native plant conservation to their bylaws.

As water use becomes more critical, you will find that to have a successful and beautiful garden, you've got to use native plants. Otherwise, you'll continue to lose shade trees, lawns, shrubs, and other mainstays of your landscape. And the gardens in your area won't have enough biodiversity to stave off epidemics of plant diseases or insect invasions that chemical warfare cannot solve.

In a garden that imitates the principles of nature, there is balance and beauty; most problems take care of themselves. So, stop fighting Mother Nature and let her do your gardening for you. She's the best gardener of all.

~

All or Nothing?

~

Sally

My sister-in-law shocked me one day. She told me that she really liked native plants but she wasn't going to use them in her landscape. She simply didn't want to give up all those other plants she also loved.

That really brought me up short. When and how had I given her the idea that using natives was an all-or-nothing proposition? And, how many others had I inadvertently infected with that silly notion? It made me realize that when a person has access to the public via the printed page or the airwaves, there's no telling how much mischief can be created.

Well, I immediately started mentally rummaging through the articles and books I'd written, the talks I'd given before garden clubs and environmental groups, and even conversations—casual and business—I'd had with clients and friends. And, honestly, nowhere, no how, no way, to the best of my recollection, had I ever stated that if you used natives you had to get rid of all of your other beloved plants. That just wouldn't make sense in landscapes, like hers, where many nonnative, but well-adapted, plants are already well established.

My philosophy has always been to use what works. The landscape I designed for Andy and me when we lived in Dallas was about 50 percent native—that is, indigenous to an area approximately fifty miles from our home. The rest were naturalized plants and a few cultivars of more exotic origin or plants native to other parts of Texas. Some of the nonnatives were there when we moved in. I added a few others myself to see how they'd do.

But, at the same time, I *do* think that there are instances where going 100 percent native makes a lot of sense. For example: When you build a home on a beautiful, untouched lot, the only sensible thing to do is to preserve that beauty. Why add a bunch of incongruous plants that are on sale at the local nursery and mess up a gorgeous landscape that is already installed and taking care of itself very nicely, thank you? If you want petunias and tomato plants, group them together in a courtyard, not out in the wild garden.

Another time you might choose to go 100 percent native is if you build on abandoned farmland that is overrun with weeds and alien invaders (plants, not Martians). You don't want to water, mow, and tend several acres! Getting rid of the weeds and re-creating a natural landscape (prairie, savanna, or woodland) that might have been there originally can be a very exciting and rewarding experience. There's the joy of finding plant treasures to add to your landscape or discovering those that magically arrive on their own. The wildlife and the marvelous complexity of nature that appears is a year-round treat.

Re-creating a natural landscape is a relatively new way of looking at gardening. Famed landscape architect Jens Jensen is credited with re-creating prairie gardens in city parks and residences in and around Chicago in the early 1900s, although he may not actually have done so. While he certainly used prairie flowers and trees, researchers have found no evidence that he planted any native prairie grasses. So we might have to go to the 1930s, when the University of Wisconsin at Madison re-created a prairie and three kinds of native Wisconsin woodlands, to find the first human-designed totally native plant landscapes.

You don't need several acres to have a natural landscape. Both prairies and forests are possible in established urban or suburban neighborhoods. They can be as small as a few hundred square feet.

If, however, you live in a neighborhood of control freaks or you're married to one, you can use natives in a more conventional design: Natives are well suited to all sorts of garden styles, even, believe it or not, formal ones. You can have parterres, allées, and symmetrical plantings if you, or your gardener, enjoy the pruning, hedging, weeding, and trimming that such designs dictate.

If you have a conventional landscape that you already enjoy, think of native plants as hardy, beautiful additions to your garden. When those not-so-well-adapted trees, shrubs, and flowers die off in droughts, freezes, and infestations, replace them with native plants.

The good news is, we're seeing more and more natives on the market these days. Growers are now providing a gorgeous array of carefully selected specimens, as well as some hybrids and cultivars that retain all of their native vigor. Added bonuses include longer flowering periods, stronger stems, or bigger blooms.

A minister I know once said, "When you're dogmatic, you paint yourself into an intellectual corner." I agree. Enjoy the rich diversity that native plants have to offer. But, when you have nonnative plants that also do well in your area, by all means use and enjoy them, too. The only exceptions are those nonnatives that are unsettlingly well adapted—so well adapted that they've become known as "invasives." More on them later.

~

When a Native Isn't

~

Sally

The term "native," when it applies to people, can get pretty sticky—we move around too much, and always have. Am I a "native Texan" because I was born in Texas? According to ordinary usage of the term, I am. Andy's ancestors have been Polish for uncounted generations, and Andy was actually born in Poland, but he is a native U.S. citizen because his father was born in America.

"Native" refers to origins. Usually it means *where* an organism evolved and developed its distinctive characteristics. Because evolution is a continuous process, *time* also has to be in the definition. At what point in evolutionary development has an organism changed enough to be called a different species?

Take, for example, humans. In the long view, and with political boundaries out of the equation, you could even question whether Native Americans are native to the Americas, or Europeans are native to Europe, as we all originally evolved in Africa and migrated to other continents.

The usual definition of a native American plant is that the plant must have been growing on its own in the Americas when Columbus landed.

This is an artificial cutoff date, but useful in separating out the plants that had been in the Americas since the last Ice Age from those brought over since 1492.

Most of our native plants have been here hundreds of thousands to millions of years. The Southern magnolia, for example, has spent all its evolutionary history on American soil, but it's moved from Utah to the Gulf Coast and changed enough to be classified as a different species from its ancestors that lived millions of years ago in what used to be steamy tropical Utah.

But some plants probably came over from Asia with the earliest American humans. Undoubtedly, some traversed the Bering Strait land bridge in the stomachs of modern bison, elk, mule deer, and other animals that were not native in Pleistocene America. That invasion that ended the Pleistocene in North America made significant changes. It marked the extinction of the mastodons, camels, horses, and giant sloths that were the native American megafauna when humans first arrived. It seems likely that many plants associated with these animals also suffered. One illustration of this is a tree in Latin America that had been dependent on the native American horse to eat and disperse its seed. After the American horse become extinct 10,000 to 12,000 years ago, the tree's range dwindled and it was almost extinct itself until saved by the horses brought over by the Spanish.

There is much we do not know. How quickly can a plant evolve? If white yarrow migrated from Siberia only 12,000 years ago, it seems it has not evolved enough solid differences to be considered a separate species from its Siberian cousin. And yet, yellow columbines, isolated into widely separated canyons by warmer and drier climates since the last Ice Age 12,000 years ago, have evolved enough visible differences to be classified as three distinct species. (Interestingly, if you plant all three in a garden, they instantly interbreed and become indistinguishable.)

On the other hand, the horsetails (*Equisetum* spp.) were prominent plants on Earth's original one continent Pangaea hundreds of millions of years ago. Since then, Pangaea has divided into all our present continents, taking horsetails with them. Most of the family is now extinct, but the horsetails in North America, Europe, and Asia are identical and also native to their respective continents. Did these plants quit evolving millions of years ago?

Fact is, all plants—except for a handful of man-made hybrids such as tea roses and most of our food crops—are natives. The question is, native to where? Some people think tulips are native to Holland; they are certainly synonymous with that lowland country. In fact, tulips originated in the

Middle East and Asia. Tomatoes, which are the mainstay of Italian cooking, didn't appear in Europe until after Columbus. Tomatoes are native to South America. And tumbleweed, which has long been linked in story and song with the American West, is actually Russian thistle and is native to Siberia.

When a plant is not native to a specific locale but acts like it is, it's called "naturalized." A naturalized plant evolved in an environment similar to its new home, so it is able to survive nicely in the wild. No matter how a naturalized plant arrived—in a bag of cattle feed, on the bottom of some pioneer's boot, or deliberately imported as an ornamental in the nursery trade—it must at some point have strayed out into the wild and survived.

Europeans, often unintentionally, started sowing American soil with foreign plants right from the beginning. In 1672, John Josselyn published his book *New England's Rarities Discovered,* in which he listed twenty-two weeds, including dandelions and plantain, which had already been introduced into the New World from Europe. Today, according to Missouri Botanical Garden, we have approximately 2,200 weeds in the continental United States—that's almost one-tenth of all our flora.

Most people have no idea which wild plants are natives and which are interlopers; some naturalized plants, however, have names that give us a good clue that they came from somewhere else: Japanese honeysuckle, Russian olive, Asiatic bittersweet, English ivy, Brazilian pepper, Australian pine, and Norway maple. Others have very misleading names, like California privet (*Ligustrum ovalifolium*). This privet is from Asia, like all of the ligustrums we use; it just entered our country through a port in California.

The ones just mentioned are invasives—weeds in the truest sense of the word—and we'll deal with them in the next chapter. Many other naturalized plants do not make pests of themselves, and can even make good companion plants in a native garden. Almost no one gets upset about blackberry lily (*Belamcanda chinensis*), jonquil (*Narcissus jonquilla*), asparagus (*Asparagus officinalis*), or watercress (*Rorippa nasturium-aquaticum*).

This might be a good time to address one of our all-time big peeves with regard to how some people—too many, I'm afraid—perceive native plants: Friends, they are not weeds!

Several years ago, Andy was on a radio program and spent the better part of an hour discussing native plants with the host. The show went well, and Andy left the studio feeling that he'd scored some big points in favor of natives and naturalistic landscaping. But when he reached the parking garage and got into his car, he got a rude awakening. The car radio was tuned to the program, and Andy heard the next guest—some comedian who was promoting his appearance at a local comedy club—say, "Well, he (Andy) can call them native plants if he wants to, but to me they're just weeds!"

When the first settlers to this country saw their first native plants, they called them "weeds." After all, these natives—forget for a moment that they were beautiful—were out there growing in the fields without any help from anyone. And they weren't familiar. Even worse, if cows, sheep, and horses didn't eat them, they were useless. So what else could they be? They had to be weeds!

There are many definitions of weeds. One of the best known comes from Ralph Waldo Emerson, who defined a weed as, "*A plant whose virtues have not yet been discovered.*"

Here's another definition: *A weed is a plant that doesn't belong.* I think this must be the subconscious definition; why else would folks spend so much time on their knees digging them out, and endangering their health by spraying all those toxins on them?

Andy says that if you buy this last definition, then simple logic dictates that a native plant *cannot* be a weed. Because what belongs to a site more than a plant that has inhabited it for thousands of years?

We rest our case.

"They planted this kudzu for erosion control. Must be workin'
because we haven't slid into the Gulf of Mexico yet!"

~

Attack of the
Killer Artichokes

~

Andy

I f you thought Sigourney Weaver had her hands full combating those metallic, drooling space monsters in the *Alien* movies, that ain't nuthin' compared to what we're facing in this country. I'm talking about invasive plants.

I can see a grin forming on your face. Did I say invasive *plants*? Yes, I did. And, unlike Seymour's voracious Venus flytrap in *Little Shop of Horrors*, or the ravenous beefsteak tomatoes in *Attack of the Killer Tomatoes*, these invading flora are nothing to laugh at!

One example:

In the 1890s, a lady from Florida visited the Louisiana Exposition and brought home a souvenir—a beautiful South American water hyacinth. She planted it in her backyard water garden, and before long she was awash in this aquatic herb. It was literally taking over her yard, so she pulled it up and dumped it into the St. Johns River that ran behind her home.

If she'd known the consequences of this simple act, she might have reconsidered; today Florida spends many millions of dollars a year trying to keep water hyacinth from choking its rivers, canals, and lakes.

Invasive aliens are not new. Like some of Boston's finest families, they first came over on the Mayflower—albeit in cattle feed. Today, invasive plants are all over. Hundreds of them! And they're not just a nuisance, they're a real threat to our ecosystem—and our economy. A study by the Congressional Office of Technology Assessment reported that between 1906 and 1991 invasive aliens cost American industry, agriculture, and health services a cool 97 billion dollars!

Our roadsides have been under siege by invasives for years. Road building rearranges and disturbs the soil. As a result, the dirt around a newly built road is susceptible to erosion. Often it is subsoil, not topsoil, and no native seeds are present. The highway department wisely learned to plant seeds that would quickly germinate and hold the soil. Their techniques are now being used to prevent erosion after forest fires and in mine reclamation projects.

Are they planting native seeds? Of course not. Even now when there is native seed available, if you require vast quantities, the cheapest prices are for agricultural seeds—usually grass seeds—that were chosen from foreign continents to revegetate hay meadows after the native prairie had been grazed to death. They are mostly cool season grasses that know how to germinate in cool soil and grab all the moisture and nutrients. So once these agricultural grasses are established, the native grasses and flowers can't come in and reclaim their native ground.

Most of you undoubtedly thought you were seeing native vegetation along our roadsides. No way! From the point of view of a native plant advocate, the majority of roadside plants are invasive weeds.

But there are also plants that farmers call weeds. Sacks of agricultural seed from Europe and Asia contain Eurasian farm weeds. There are not very many per sack, but even one or two seeds can germinate, and the cows and their calves won't eat them. So their seed ripens and scatters and germinates and the next year there are dozens more of this unpalatable plant for the cattle to avoid and thousands more of its seed self-sows, and in a few years, those one or two seeds have taken over the field.

The trouble is, most invasives are attractive and don't look threatening. Incredibly, many are actually sold in nurseries as ornamentals. The thing is, if these plants would just stay put in our gardens—the way other imported exotics do—they'd be welcome. But they escape and, because they lack the natural controls they had at home (browsers, disease, etc.), they run amok.

Take crown vetch, which comes from Asia and North Africa. Driving along a highway in Canada a few years back, we saw mile after mile of this pink groundcover—very likely planted by the highway department. I'm sure most people comment on how pretty it is. But what they're admiring is a monoculture—one plant that takes over, crowding out dozens of native species that *should* be growing there, and destroying valuable wildlife habitats in the process.

In the Southwest, roadsides are glutted with black mustard from Eurasia. In the Northeast and Midwest, garlic mustard, buckthorn, and purple loosestrife are major problems, as is birds-foot trefoil, deliberately introduced from Europe as livestock fodder.

In southern California, wild artichoke from the Mediterranean has become an agricultural pest. And throughout much of that state, blue eucalyptus from Australia is so common, many residents think it is native. Aside from crowding out native species, it poses a real fire hazard; it's a messy tree, and produces a great deal of combustible litter—bark, small limbs, and oily leaves. (Amazingly, there is an active organization dedicated to promoting this invasive— it's called POET, for Protect Our Eucalyptus Trees!)

So, you ask: Why doesn't our government do something? Ah, but you see, the government is a big part of the problem.

On the one hand, they've started an expensive campaign to help rid our roadsides, ranches, and farms of invasive weeds like thistles. Full-color brochures are being printed to show the public which plants are to be killed. Lots of taxpayer money is being handed out to spray glysophate and other Monsanto-produced herbicides. Nonpoisonous solutions advocate grazing goats or frequent mowing. Unfortunately, all these methods kill beneficial native plants along with the weeds. Furthermore, there is no discrimination between the noninvasive native thistles that host butterflies and finches and the invasive nonnative thistles, as cattle can't eat any of them.

But this is just one of our federal agencies. With the other hand, the Feds are actively encouraging citizens to plant invasives. Federal agencies and state highway departments are handing out Siberian elm and Russian olive to ranchers in the Dakotas and Montana to be used as windbreaks. Thanks to Uncle Sam's largesse, these trees now infest waterways from Canada all the way down into Texas. You'd think he might have learned a lesson from his fiasco with Asian kudzu. In the 1920s, our government promoted it for erosion control. Today kudzu is called "the vine that ate the South!" Of course, one can argue that the strategy was successful—Alabama hasn't slipped into the Gulf of Mexico yet. (A few years ago, Sally gave a talk to a garden club and addressed the subject of invasives. As she was leaving, a lady followed her out to her car and asked if Sally knew where she could get some of that beautiful kudzu.)

Another problem is nurseries. Many of these invasives are actually sold to the public as ornamentals. Recently, while attending a conference in Albuquerque, I called eight nurseries and asked if they carried Russian olive. Yes, they all replied. Did they know, I pressed on, that these trees were invasive and a threat to the environment? Yes, they responded. Then why, I asked, do you sell them? The answer I got was staggering. Oh, we're just giving the public what they want. Really? Isn't that the same rationale you'd get from a drug dealer?

I tried this in Houston, asking about Chinese tallow (popcorn tree), and along the East Coast, asking about Chinese privet. The answers I got were remarkably similar.

Here and there we see a ray of hope: In many states in the Northeast, it is now illegal to sell purple loosestrife and Santa Fe, New Mexico, recently passed an ordinance forbidding nurseries to sell Russian olive. But that's a drop in the bucket. People, this is war—and we'd better recognize the problem and act now—before we're all up to our eyeballs in aliens!

Of course, we have already changed the evolutionary gene pool of our continent forever. But there are steps worth taking to stem the invasion, without resorting to poisons that hurt the soil and everything that grows in it. We can employ work crews to weed out every invasive plant and burn it. We can restore some degree of annual flooding to floodplains, allowing cottonwoods and willows to make a comeback. We can stop planting invasive plants and start planting natives. Sally's theory is that if we put as much time, effort, and money into restoring native plants over the next 150 years as we put into destroying them and planting nonnative plants over the last 150 years, the natives could make a comeback.

Want to know more about invasive aliens and how to combat them? Janet Marinelli and John M. Randall put together a terrific book profiling seventy-five of our worst invaders—most of them sold commercially. To get a copy, contact the Brooklyn Botanic Garden and order their handbook, *Invasive Plants: Weeds of the Global Garden*, ISBN 0-945352-95-6. Contact them at 1000 Washington Ave., Brooklyn, NY 11225, or call them at 718-623-7200.

Another book to consider is *Alien Invasion: America's Battle with Non-Native Animals and Plants* by Robert S. Devine, ISBN 0-7922-74490.

Oh, and, Sigourney, if you're not too busy, we could use a little help.

5

An Eskimo in Death Valley

Sally

I was born and raised in Texas, which means I grew up used to lots of sunshine and warmth. For a few years I lived in New York and Illinois and experienced "real" winters; I was miserable. I was out of my provenance.

Andy was born and raised in northern climes; he loves winter and lots of snow and is beyond cranky when the temperature rises above ninety. He complained one August day that he "felt like an Eskimo in Death Valley!" Clearly in Texas, he was out of *his* provenance.

Provenance is the Anglicized version of a Latin word that means roughly, "from whence it came." At this point, you're probably thinking, "Who cares?" Well, if you buy plants and you want them to be healthy, you should care a lot.

When we talk about the provenance of, for example, a live oak, we aren't referring to the species *Quercus virginiana* as a whole (and about six others, depending on whose nomenclature you follow). We're talking about one particular live oak tree. The one at your local nursery, the one over by the fence, the one you're thinking about buying. You may know that live oaks in general are native from the southern Atlantic coast to central Texas and Oklahoma. But that isn't the same as knowing that this particular live oak tree, with its own unique set of genes, is native right around where you live.

Why is this important to know? Let's use Dallas as an example; we were living there during the winter of 1983–1984 and saw this firsthand. We were deep-freeze city. (I don't expect any sympathy from you folks in Montana and Minnesota, but believe me, for Texans, it was coooold!) Half of our live oaks popped their barks and died. That half included those trees sent here from growers in Houston and southern Louisiana. The other half—the ones that were totally *un*damaged—came from growers in neighboring Fort Worth.

If you're getting ready to spend about $1,500 for a live oak or a maple or whatever, it sure would be nice to know that your tree had the right provenance for your brand of winters.

But provenance affects more than winter-hardiness. Drought and summer-hardiness are also important. Possumhaw (*Ilex decidua*) is a gorgeous ornamental tree that is native from Virginia to Illinois and down to the Gulf of Mexico; the female is ablaze with red berries from November through March when the new leaves appear. Now, let's say you live in the westernmost part of a possumhaw's native range in the Texas Hill Country. And you see that your local nurseries are carrying a number of selections—some with yellow berries, some with orange, some with bigger berries, and so on.

But, suppose those nursery clones were developed from possumhaws that are native to the Carolinas, where the rainfall averages up to thirty inches a year *more* than it does where you live. Do you think those Carolina possumhaws are going to appreciate your arid summers and be in the pink of health? Not likely. They will be drought-stressed and hurt by insects and diseases. But the possumhaws whose provenance is Austin, Texas, will not. Unlike the imported ones, those native to your part of the country— once established—will require no maintenance except for an occasional bit of cosmetic pruning. And they are equally varied and pretty.

The calendar itself can spell disaster for a plant of the wrong provenance, specifically during the first wintry storm in the fall and in the first false flush of spring. This is because plants have two main mechanisms for figuring out when winter and spring are coming for real.

Some plants are light sensitive. As the days become shorter, they quit growing, send sap down to their roots for safekeeping, and get all battened down for winter. A red oak from hardiness Zone 7 should certainly be winter-hardy in Zone 8, right? Maybe not, because the days get shorter earlier in Zone 7. This red oak will keep growing and waiting for the short-day signal and get caught by a blue norther. It will never get a chance to have beautiful red fall color, and it might suffer severe freeze damage, even though it could endure much colder winter temperatures.

Northern-selected fruit trees get their flowers nipped in the spring for the same reason; longer days in the South fool them into thinking that spring is further along than it really is.

The other way plants try to tell the seasons is by temperature. If they expect a gradual cooling during the days and 40° to 50°F nights to give them a clue that winter is coming, they can be caught entirely by surprise in the Great Plains area where temperatures can plummet with no warning.

For a plant (especially a tree that is supposed to live for decades or even centuries) to withstand all of the vagaries that the weather might produce, it needs to have genes honed by those weather patterns. Otherwise, some year, a winter storm or a summer drought will damage it.

So, before you buy, make sure your plant is right for your climate. Purchase a plant whose provenance is within one hundred miles of where you live. Ask the people at your nursery. If they don't know, they should be able to find out for you. If they can't, try another nursery. Independent nursery owners are usually the most knowledgeable, and independent native plant nursery owners have often hand-gathered the seed or cuttings themselves.

PART II

Zeroing in on Your Own Backyard

My first bit of advice to people determined to attempt things reluctant to thrive on an unsuitable soil would be: Don't. It is much better to stick to the things that happen to like the kind of soil you have got in your garden and give other things a miss. I know this is a hard saying, cutting out a whole lot of temptations, but I am sure it is a right one. It is not good trying to force plants to adopt a way of life they don't like; they just won't have it unless you are rich enough to undertake excavations the size of a quarry.

—VITA SACKVILLE-WEST

A Brief History
of the 'Burbs

Andy

Suburbia and the lawn-centered landscape are, for the most part, insep-
arable. Today, one can travel from the Atlantic to the Pacific coasts,
from Canada down into Texas or Florida, and see virtually that same
landscape replicated block after block, neighborhood after neighborhood.

But where did the suburbs come from? And how did we get stuck with
those high-maintenance, water-sucking landscapes?

An ancient Chinese general once said, "*Know your enemy, know yourself. A thousand battles, a thousand victories.*" Since we in the native plant
movement hope to achieve victory over the suburban landscape in the not-
too-distant future, it might be a good idea to look at the origins of suburbia and the ubiquitous suburban front and backyard.

Mention the suburbs and most people probably think of the great
housing boom that followed World War II. But in fact we had suburbs a
lot earlier than that.

The word *suburbis* was used by John Wycliffe as early as 1380, and Chaucer introduced the term in a dialogue in *The Canterbury Tales* a few years later. By 1500 extramural parishes were designed as London suburbs, and by the seventeenth century the adjective *suburban* was being used to mean both the place and the person who lived there.

Here in America, Boston, Philadelphia, and New York had established suburbs well before the Revolutionary War. In 1719, one John Staniford advertised a new real estate development at Barton's Point, Massachusetts, as "*laid out in House Lotts with two Streets Cross, that have a very find prospect upon the River and Charlestown and a great part of Boston.*"

But the term goes still further back. Open your King James Bible to The Book of Joshua, chapter 21, and you'll read, "*Thus they gave to the children of Aaron the priest Hebron with her suburbs. . . .*"

But the most interesting reference to suburbs that I came across was in the book *Crabgrass Frontier: The Suburbanization of the United States* by Kenneth T. Jackson. In it, Jackson quotes from a letter written to a friend in the city about the writer's new life in suburbia. The writer didn't actually use that term, but read this excerpt and see if it doesn't sound like the ideal of suburban living: "*Our property seems to me the most beautiful in the world. It is so close to (the city) that we enjoy all the advantages of the city, and yet when we come home we are away from all the noise and dust.*"

This letter was written on a clay tablet in 539 B.C., and the city referred to was Babylon!

In the mid-nineteenth century, suburbs were springing up around virtually every American city and large town. Admittedly, they were small compared to post-1945, and residents didn't have to travel for miles on congested highways to get home. Usually they could stroll home for lunch from their shops and offices, which were just a few blocks away "downtown."

Some yards were filled with English-style flower gardens—usually very formal and composed of imported exotics from the Old World. But, for the most part, these homeowners didn't have a clue what to do with their yards, and so they left them bare.

It wasn't until 1870 that they got the word. Cincinnati landscape architect Frank J. Scott wrote a book titled *The Art of Beautifying Suburban Home Grounds,* and it became a bestseller. In it, Scott (no relation to the seed company) told his readers that "*A smooth, closely shaven surface of grass is by far the most essential element of beauty on the grounds of a suburban home.*" America's homeowners readily accepted his views, and we've been stuck with mowing and edging and all those other chores ever since.

By the time Scott's book came out, we already had the tools we needed to follow his advice. In 1830, an English textile engineer named Edward Budding observed a rotary shear used to trim the nap on carpet and dreamed up the lawnmower. The first American patent was issued in 1868, and by the end of the nineteenth century we had the first power mowers, the roars of which have been disturbing our Saturday mornings ever since. The year after Scott's book came out, the first U.S. patent was issued for the lawn sprinkler.

Interestingly, early in the twentieth century, the spread of lawns was closely tied to the growing popularity of golf. The "perfect lawn" concept arose when amateur golfers noticed the well-maintained greens upon which they drove, chipped, and putted, and began to develop higher standards for their own home turf. For landscaping advice they turned, not to professional landscapers or gardeners, but to the managers of their local golf courses. A 1926 ad for Toro equipment suggested that readers "ask the Greenskeeper at your own course what he thinks of Toro equipment." Other lawn care ads promoted the "golf course look" as the ideal for suburban homes, and PGA stars such as Sam Snead and Bobby Jones (and later Arnold Palmer and Jack Nicklaus) touted lawn care products in magazines and on TV.

During World War II, Americans were deprived of much of the help they'd become used to from the lawn care industry. Lawnmower manufacturers were making equipment for the armed forces, fertilizer companies were making munitions, and the makers of lawn chemicals were playing with poison gas. But they didn't want us to forget their products, so they continued to advertise. One ad proclaimed, "Your 1943 Coldwell mower is riding the convoy lanes somewhere on the high seas." But they added, "The new ideas and methods we are learning every day assure you of the finest lawnmowers obtainable in the future."

After the war, suburbia really took off as millions of servicemen and -women returned to find the good life, and real estate developers such as William Levitt began mass-producing suburban cookie-cutter homes, each with its "picture perfect" lawn. We were on the way to our present lawn-o-mania.

And not a moment too soon, lamented an article in *Home and Garden* magazine. In it they expressed the rather bizarre notion that "The lawn is one of the saddest wartime casualties."

❧

7

Taking a Regional View

❧

Sally

Over the years Andy and I have lived together or singly in many states, from New York to New Mexico and from California to Alabama. But one state stands out in our minds as unique—at least from a botanical perspective—Texas. No other state can boast such an incredible diversity of terrain, climates, rainfalls, and soils. (Californians may dispute this, but then tell me why so many movie producers go on location in Texas?)

Look at it this way: Texas is the United States in microcosm. Want rugged mountains? Or a true desert? They've got 'em. Not to mention seashores and cypress swamps, eastern pine forests, midwestern oak savannas, southwestern juniper savannas, tallgrass prairies, shortgrass prairies, coastal prairies, and desert grasslands. And each specific set of conditions is host to a colorful array of native plants that thrive there—and sometimes only there.

Notice, I'm talking about regions, not states. States are artificial, man-made contrivances, and plants don't pay much attention to lines on maps. For although all of the plant communities in Texas, except for the fabled

Texas Hill Country, overlap the state's boundaries into adjoining states or Mexico, these habitats are a little different in Texas than they are anywhere else. For example: tallgrass prairie in Illinois is similar to tallgrass prairie in Texas, but detailed plant lists and bloom times differ enough to make a prairie restoration in Illinois totally inappropriate for a prairie restoration in Texas.

Take a plant such as big bluestem (*Andropogon gerardii*). It's the dominant plant in both Illinois and Texas tallgrass prairies. However, in Illinois it can grow over six feet tall, while in Texas I've never seen it over four feet, even in flower. In Illinois, its codominant grasses might be Indiangrass, little bluestem, and switchgrass (the same as in Texas) but it might also be codominant with prairie dropseed (which doesn't grow within several hundred miles of Texas.) Furthermore, seed from an Illinois big bluestem is not adapted to Texas summer heat.

And this is really the point. You have to know what works where you are. Sagebrush that thrives in Teasdale, Utah, for example, would rot in the humidity of Bucksnort, Tennessee. Even if it were possible—and ultimately, it really isn't—we wouldn't want Teasdale to look like Bucksnort—and vice versa.

It's that unique sense of time and place and local character that fosters pride in an area. And, much of that uniqueness comes from the native plant life. Ideally, local plants should interact with the local architecture and create a harmonious, natural ambience.

Picture a lovely Southern antebellum home complete with a two-story columned porch. Now, envision it surrounded by live oaks draped in Spanish moss, palmettos, and southern magnolias. This is a landscape that looks right at home along the Gulf Coast. But, imagine that house and landscape outside of, say, Tucson, Arizona. The scene would be so jarringly out of context in that Southwestern setting—well, it would make your teeth hurt!

In the Southwest, a dazzling, neon bright lawn looks garish and out of sorts with the muted desert greens that range from soft yellows to pale blues and silvers. Instead, you'd want a lovely desert home built in the Spanish style, probably adobe, and you'd surround it with green-trunked, yellow-flowered paloverde trees, yuccas, cacti, bursage, and pink penstemons. That's a naturally lovely scene for that part of the country. The only thing missing would be The Sons of the Pioneers singing *Cool Water* in the background.

Each landscape, in its proper setting, needs a minimum of water and maintenance to look its best. But, each would be an immense amount of trouble, if not impossible to accomplish, on the other's home ground. Yet I've seen any number of landscapes just as incongruous. Would you believe banana trees in Oklahoma?

We human animals persist in trying to dominate our environment, to bend it to our will, and to alter it to fit our ideas. We can succeed for a time. We can use unconscionable amounts of water keeping St. Augustine and Kentucky bluegrass lawns green, when native buffalograss or blue grama would look just as lush with a fraction of that water. We can truck in soils and hope to fool the plants into thinking they're growing in sandy loam when in fact they're on limestone or in clay. And, we can spend inordinate amounts of money on fertilizers, trying to maintain these interlopers, herbicides to quell the competition, and pesticides and fungicides to keep them alive.

In the end, of course, we are going to fail. The imported plants will die in droughts with which they aren't genetically able to cope. The late freezes will damage the alien trees and shrubs that haven't learned to wait out these tricks of nature.

And, guess what? The public (not you, of course) will go out to their nurseries and buy the exact same plants, trying once again to make them live where Mother Nature never intended them to be in the first place.

You know the old adage: "If at first you don't succeed, try, try again." When it comes to gardening, however, the adage ought to read, "If at first you don't succeed, maybe Mother Nature is trying to tell you something."

8

~

Can You Say Xeriscape?

~

Sally and Andy

With all the work the Denver Water Department has to do, you wouldn't think they'd have had time to dabble in lexicology. Back in the early 1980s, however, they, along with Colorado's landscape industry, came up with a program to assist homeowners in reducing water consumption, and then coined a new word for this program: *xeriscape* (the *x* is pronounced like a *z*). The word comes from the Greek root word *xeros*, meaning "dry."

Literally then, xeriscaping means "dry landscaping." Unfortunately, some people take that to mean a barebones landscape—"*zero*-scaping!"—that consists of gravel, a lava rock or two, and a few yuccas. This is sometimes referred to as the "Sun City" look, which is really a caricature of a true desert landscape. (In order to conserve water, some folks take other measures: A homeowner in El Paso, Texas, covered his front yard with astroturf, while a lady in Albuquerque, New Mexico, replaced her bedding plants with plastic and silk flowers!)

In fact, having a xeriscape simply means using those plants that can exist on whatever rainfall you normally get. If you live in southern Louisiana

"Okay, you can water the lawn today,
but I get to bathe the kids tomorrow."

where you can get upwards of fifty inches per annum, you can have a xeriscape using plants that are native to your part of the state that would be water-guzzlers elsewhere: spiderlily, pickerelweed, dwarf palmetto, bushy bluestem, arrowwood, southern magnolia . . . you've got a lot of options.

New concepts don't take hold overnight (We understand that there is still an active Flat-Earth Society out there), and we have to report that xeriscaping is not yet a household word. You can still receive vacant stares when you mention it to most people. And, I don't know of anyone who has used it in a Scrabble game. Okay, so call it waterwise gardening or whatever sounds best to you. The point is, the basic concept *is* becoming popular with a growing number of professional landscapers and home gardeners alike who are concerned with water conservation. And since water shortages are not limited to deserts, water departments all over the country are also promoting the principles of xeriscaping and sending out xeriscaping information along with their bills; you've probably received at least one.

There's a lot more to xeriscaping than simply using native plants. A major part of the program consists of encouraging folks to—are you ready for this?—get rid of their lawns. Or at the very least greatly reduce lawn areas. We pointed out earlier that lawns can consume from 40 to 60 percent of household water. We once talked to an employee of the Water Department in Palm Springs and were told that this figure can go as high as 80 percent in the summer.

And that translates into a lot of water! According to figures supplied by the EPA, a twenty-five feet by forty-feet lawn requires 10,000 gallons each summer to stay green, and 12,000 gallons if you insist on a "bouncy, vibrant green" look. But there are many who say these figures are way too low. The Denver Water Department reported on annual water consumption in that city and found that an average household (2.7 people) uses 132,000 gallons of water per year. And of that, approximately half (66,000 gallons) is used for outdoor purposes—washing the car, the kids' water slide, and of course, watering the lawn—which alone accounts for over 90 percent of that outdoor water use. That's over 59,000 gallons per household. Moreover, when they surveyed a dozen cities across the country in a wide range of climates, from Tampa to Seattle, they found the numbers still higher. On average, 184,000 gallons were consumed per household, 90,000 gallons of which were poured on lawns!

As you may have gathered by now, we are not big fans of lawns. Aside from being incorrigible drinkers, we think they're basically pretty boring. But, if you insist on having a lawn around your home, you have two options: If you live anywhere from southern Canada down to northern Texas, and between the Rockies and the Mississippi River, you can probably use native buffalograss (see chapter 23, "Grass Roots Support for Buffalograss") which uses a fraction of the water needed by Kentucky blue, Bermuda, and most other conventional turf grasses. Your second option, no matter what kind of lawn you have, is to care for it with some basic water-conserving techniques.

We can't remember how many times we've driven through neighborhoods in states where there are serious water problems and seen sprinklers going full blast at noon. Much of that precious water runs off into the streets and is wasted. Another large percentage of it simply evaporates under the summer sun.

In the early 1990s, Joe Henggeler, Extension Agriculture Engineer of Irrigation in Fort Stockton, Texas, did some studies on water loss in home landscapes. He found that only 10 percent of water loss is the visible part we see running down streets and sidewalks. Forty percent can be blamed on wind drift and evaporation and another 40 percent on overwatering where water soaks in beneath the root zone. In a volunteer two-year program in Fort Stockton and Andrews, it was found that some homeowners had been overwatering by 300 percent, simply because they weren't adjusting their sprinkler systems for seasonal differences. For example, eight inches of water might be necessary for a lush garden in July, but one-half inch might be sufficient in March. Some homeowners were watering eight inches *every month!*

An important, but often overlooked, way of cutting water bills involves the proper adjustment of the timer on a sprinkler system. Most home sprinkler systems are divided into zones, with each zone designed to cover its particular part of the landscape. That's why each zone varies in number of heads, head type, pressure, and flow rate. But, setting the timer for the *same* number of minutes for each zone may in fact *overwater* one zone and *underwater* another. According to Henggeler's studies, making sure each zone gets just the right amount and *no more* can save up to 40 percent of your costs.

Other tips for sensible watering:

- It should always be done in the coolest parts of the day, preferably after sundown.
- Water in two short cycles instead of one long one to reduce runoff. Better yet, use a drip irrigation or bubbler system; it's far more efficient.

- Water deeply. When the water gets down to a depth of four to six inches, the roots are encouraged to grow down deeper, where it stays moist longer.
- Aerate the soil for better water penetration.
- Use mulches, such as bark chips and straw, around trees and shrubs. They keep the roots cool and cut evaporation by as much as 70 percent.
- Check your watering or irrigation system for leaks. Even a teeny one can waste incredible amounts of water.

Of course, the most important step is to use native or well-adapted exotics that can survive without supplemental water at all.

So, how much water would actually get saved if everyone went xeriscapic? That's the difficult part. As we've seen, responsible agencies can't agree on how much water we consume. Moreover, as each family is different, so too would be the approach they take to xeriscaping. Did they get rid of all their lawn, or just most of it? Are all their plants drought tolerant, or did they keep a few tropicals? What kind of irrigation system are they using? Is it in good repair, or does it leak like a dribble glass? Soils also differ—clay holds water while sandy loam drains quickly. You also need to factor in what part of the country you live in. Arid desert? Rainy southland? Wind can also be a factor; strong and constant winds such as many parts of the country experience can evaporate a lot of water.

Okay, so let's say that on average xeriscaping cuts outdoor water consumption in half. (Actually, some experts believe it's a lot more than that.) That would be 45,000 gallons per household annually. Not counting apartments and condos, the U.S. Census Bureau tells us there are some 65 million single-family homes in this country—virtually all still with lawns. So multiply that by 45,000 and you've got almost 3 trillion gallons saved each year. You could float a small navy in that much water.

࿘

Danger in Your Bookstore

࿘

Sally

Beware. Danger lurks in your bookstore's gardening section. No, I don't mean a 4-lb. edition of *The Gardener's Desk Reference* is likely to topple down on you from the top shelf; I'm referring to the misinformation you're likely to pick up from perfectly nice, well-meaning, and extremely knowledgeable gardening authors.

The first thing you have to understand about the gardening section of your bookstore is that only a miniscule percentage of the books will be about plants native or even suited to your part of the country—maybe three or four titles out of a hundred. The rest deal with conventional nursery stock and traditional gardening methods: how to grow bigger and better hostas, how to install an English border garden, how to cultivate the perfect beefsteak tomatoes, and so on. These books are marketed to the entire country so, in most cases, the information is generalized—sort of a one-size-fits-all approach—and this can often be misleading.

Also, although I haven't actually done a scientific study on this, it's our impression that a large percentage of the authors live either in New England and New York or along the Pacific Coast. Certainly that's where most of the publishers are located. And, sometimes they forget about those of us who live out in the vast hinterlands in between. They forget that what works so well for them may not work for us at all.

Remember that classic Steinberg poster showing the United States as seen from New York City? In the foreground we see the Hudson River, off on the horizon is California, and in the middle of the picture is this blank gray area—where most of the rest of us reside.

What brought this to mind was that I was recently rereading a book on trees by one of America's foremost plant gurus. I'm a great admirer of his work and one of his books is among my best references.

But I could not be as enthusiastic about his tree guide. This "definitive" work contains detailed entries for over 1,100 recommended trees, along with a list of 1,300 "inferior" species and varieties. When I first encountered this book, I was living and working as a landscape designer in Dallas, and I couldn't help but notice that only a handful of his recommended trees were suitable for use in Texas. There are probably only a handful suitable for where you live, too.

The thing is, you'd never know from looking through this book which trees you ought to use and which ones you ought to avoid. Without any other, more localized, information as a guide, a homeowner living in that "blank gray area" would dutifully purchase and plant countless trees that do very well in Massachusetts. These trees, magnificent choices for much of the Northeastern United States, are disasters elsewhere. They develop molds and fungi in the humid Deep South. They consume too much water in arid regions where they succumb to summer heat, saline water, and differently timed freezes. As they become stressed, they fall prey to a wide range of diseases and insects.

If you live in the Southwest or the Mountain West, most of the best trees for you aren't even mentioned in this book, because they couldn't live in Massachusetts long enough to be tested.

I don't mean to single out one author; this kind of thing is all too common in far too many gardening books that purport to talk to a national market. These books are written by those who have not lived in enough parts of the country to understand that each place has its own special needs and conditions. I'm convinced that those gardeners who live around New York City are the most provincial in the country. (Notable exceptions to this rule are Janet Marinelli, Ken Druse, and Sara Stein.)

A few years ago, another popular garden book writer from the East was in Dallas on a promotional tour for her latest book. Andy caught her on a local call-in talk show, and the program was really an eye-opener. The callers asked her specific how-to questions, and her responses were more often than not, "Well, you'd better ask your local nursery about that." Really? Well, lady, why should we buy your book if you don't know any more about us than that?

Until recently, this type of gardening book was all that was available. This has influenced not only the nursery industry, but also landscape architects and, therefore, all the public landscapes we see.

For a brief while, it appeared that publishers were waking up to the need for regional gardening books. However, there have been recent convulsions in the book business. More and more small publishers are being bought up by giant publishing houses that are so large they don't even know what books they have. (The present publisher of this book is a happy exception.)

What we need are regional divisions that focus on the needs of their region. We need gardening books that address the unique conditions in various parts of the country and tell us, specifically, which plants do best in which regions of each state. We need more gardening authors like Bob Perry in southern California, Judith Phillips in New Mexico, and Leonard Foote and Samuel Jones in the Southeast—honest-to-goodness local experts who actually live with the plants they write about and even get their hands dirty digging in the local soils.

❧

10

Good People, Good Intentions, Bad Input

❧

Sally and Andy

ive credit where credit is due. Those folks on the extreme right of the political spectrum have a genuine talent for name-calling. Eco-freak Environmental whacko. Bleeding heart. Doom-and-gloomer. And, of course, that ever popular epithet, treehugger!

It's usually said with a sneer and an air of superiority—the implication being that anyone who expresses concern about the welfare of trees is more to be pitied than scorned. "Hey, man, trees just aren't worth that kind of energy." As a former movie actor turned President once said, "A tree is a tree. How many do you need to look at?"

Actually, the answer is—lots!

We're proud to consider ourselves dedicated treehuggers—Andy even has a T-shirt identifying him as such—and we consider people like Julia "Butterfly" Hill (who lived for two years atop a 200-foot ancient redwood to save it from the chain saws) among the real heroes of our age. Considering the environmental state of the world, we wonder why *every-one* isn't a professed treehugger. Have you ever stood next to a giant red-wood, or hiked through an old-growth forest, or flown over New England in the autumn and looked down on that mind-boggling ocean of oranges and reds and yellows?

From a purely pragmatic point of view, we *need* trees. Lots of them. Good healthy trees so that we can go on being healthy ourselves; so all that carbon dioxide being produced by cars and industry can be converted into oxygen. When Al Gore was still a senator, he wrote in his thoughtful and disturbing book, *Earth in the Balance,* "Forests represent the single most important stabilizing feature of the earth's land surface, and they cushion us from the worst effects—particularly those associated with global warming—of the environmental crisis."

The good news is that the treehugger movement is alive and well out there. Activists literally risk their lives protesting clear-cutting and the destruction of old-growth forests. From time to time, we receive newsletters from various groups, full of inspiring tales of how some small town somewhere has organized a community tree-planting effort. And it's rare to find a garden show or environmental seminar that doesn't include at least one speaker on urban and suburban reforestation. Sometimes, saplings are for sale right outside the door, discounted to encourage audiences to buy 'em and plant 'em. Some organizations will even give you a free tree if you promise to plant it and get it established.

This sounds marvelous, and at first glance we should all be glad that this movement is so aggressive and enthusiastic. We're all for planting more trees. And we're delighted to see that many others are too.

So what's wrong with this admittedly noble effort? Plenty.

Example: The National Arbor Day Foundation, of all people, recently ran an ad to attract new members. The ad presented "Ten reasons you should plant a tree . . . now!" and listed them: trees conserve energy, help clean the air, attract songbirds . . . and so on. The ad ended with an offer to send you ten flowering trees if you would send them a $10 membership contribution. The trees offered were two flowering dogwoods, two flowering crabapples, two goldenraintrees, two Washington hawthorns, and two American redbuds.

Now, as previously noted, we live in northern New Mexico. So we wondered, would they send us those trees if we joined—whether or not they were suited to where we live? Or, would anyone notice our address and offer us better options? Only one way to find out. . . .

The trees arrived in the fall—the same five listed in the ad. Flowering dogwood (*Cornus florida*) was totally wrong, not just for northern New Mexico, but the entire Southwest. It likes acid soil, and ours is alkaline. This tree is native to the eastern United States, from New England down to the Florida panhandle, and west to east Texas and on up to Indiana and Illinois.

There are several crabapples in the *Malus* family; we got *Malus ioensis*, known as the prairie crabapple, which is suitable to the Midwest.

Bougainvillea goldenraintree (*Koelreuteria bipinnata*), while native to China, will grow in our area as long as it gets sufficient water. But we live in an arid state that is going through a long-term drought; water-guzzlers are not welcome. But what if we lived in some other state—say, Ohio, Illinois, Indiana, Kentucky, Maryland, New York, North Carolina, Pennsylvania, Virginia, or West Virginia? The USDA warns that golden-raintree can escape into the wild in those states, and some people consider this tree an invasive.

Washington hawthorn (*Crataegus phaenopyrum*), a member of the rose family, will do fine in the same states as the dogwood, but not New Mexico. And the redbud (*Cercis canadensis*) is good for the eastern United States as far west as southern Michigan, southern Iowa, southern Nebraska, and eastern Texas.

We did not get an options list offering us trees that are native or at least well adapted to northern New Mexico, and unless you were a botanist, you probably wouldn't know that it mattered.

Interestingly, nowhere in the ad is the term "native tree" used.

From time to time, at various meetings and seminars, we find ourselves sharing guest-speaking chores with representatives of some of these tree-planting organizations. Again, young trees are offered to encourage plant-ing. Many, if not all, of these trees are wrong for the areas where the audiences live. When we ask the speakers about this, they appear genuinely surprised by the question; apparently it had never occurred to them that it makes any difference. What a tragedy that most of these groups are urging people to plant the *wrong* trees.

Can there be a wrong tree? Isn't any tree better than no tree? No. There are two types of wrong tree: the kind that is good in its rightful place but is ill-adapted where it is being distributed, and the kind that is short-lived and trashy no matter where you plant it. Either will take up space, water, fertilizer . . . and then in a few short years, sometimes in just a few months, waste that investment by dying and producing more methane and carbon dioxide as it rots and takes up space in a landfill.

The wrong tree makes the problem worse, not better.

Slash pines (*Pinus elliottii*), fast-growing trees that love acid soil and fifty inches of rain a year, are a good choice for the coastal plains in the Deep South, but a disaster in Oklahoma City where there is alkaline clay and limestone and rainfall averages only twenty-five to thirty-five inches a year. First the slash pines turn yellow, and then they die, however much water you give them. Yet a few years back we saw an arboretum (an *arboretum* for Pete's sake!) in just such an alkaline region handing out free slash pines to visitors.

Just west of Boulder, Colorado, on the lower slopes of the Front Range of the Rocky Mountains, ponderosa pine and Douglas fir are the two dominant trees, with Douglas fir more frequent on the north-facing slopes. You would not be doing anyone a favor by sending slash pines here.

However, ponderosa pine and Douglas fir are not going to grow just twenty miles away on the east side of Denver either, not without supplemental water. Colorado changes drastically from the dry, flat, treeless Great Plains in the east to the moist mixed conifer and aspen forests at high elevations. Just because a tree is native to a region doesn't mean it's native all over that region. Different elevations create different climates, and different climates call for different trees.

Soil types and the water table, the proximity of ground water to the surface, are also significant in determining what is the right tree for the right spot. In Wisconsin, bur oaks or white oaks are majestic on the rich well-drained soils around Milwaukee, but black oaks grow better with white pines on sandy soil, and where the water table is high, aspens are a good fast-growing choice.

Actually, distributing even the right tree in the right place in massive quantities can be dangerous. Many of the trees you buy at nurseries have been grown from cuttings or were grown from seed gathered from the same few mother trees. They are genetically akin, and are therefore vulnerable to a mass infestation of some disease or pest.

It's also important to have a variety of trees. Every forest is composed primarily of at least two species, and rich forests have dozens of species. The more variety, the less chance that one insect can wipe out significant hunks of the forest—or a large number of trees in one neighborhood.

The southern hardwood forest is the most complex and possesses the most species. It stretches from the southern foothills of the Appalachians north to eastern Minnesota and southwestern Maine, and west to the Mississippi River. According to soil and sun, the dominant trees might be white oak, chestnut oak, Spanish oak, black oak, black jack oak, post oak, willow oak, three kinds of hickories, sweet gum, beech, tulip poplar, red maple, or black gum. These are the seed- and nut-bearing canopy trees that form the roof of the forest. Under them are shorter trees that have colorful flowers and fruits, such as flowering dogwood, redbud, several kinds of magnolias, sassafras, and persimmon. Under them are tall shrubs or short multitrunked trees such as witchhazel, and numerous species of viburnums and hollies. Shrubby flowers, delicate spring bulbs, ferns, mosses, shade-tolerant grasses, and woodland sedges carpet the shadowy forest floor.

Obviously, it would be daunting, if not virtually impossible, to offer all these trees for reforestation at any one time. However, tree distributors in such rich forest areas might consider growing and offering a different, rotating selection of two or three suitable trees each year. But please remember—black oaks, for example, grown from acorns gathered in Alabama should not be planted in Maine or Minnesota. (Refer back to chapter 7, "An Eskimo in Death Valley.")

To successfully reforest America, we can't simply choose three species—or ten or even twenty-five—and send them any old place. The growing and the distribution should be localized. To insure survival through summer, winter, wet years, and dry years, the trees need to be propagated from trees that are native right in the immediate vicinity.

In our park systems, as well as other public lands, such as large school yards and along highways, the smartest, easiest, and most efficient way to increase our woodlands and ensure getting the best possible plants is also the most economical. The way to do this is to start a program of contour mowing. In the areas left unmowed, seedlings from existing trees will quickly get established, and Mother Nature will select the healthiest. After about five years, if you want a more parklike look, you can cut down excess saplings and start mowing again. However, to provide good habitat for wildlife, all parks should establish permanent lines of contour mowing that leave large areas untouched and wild.

Urban and suburban reforestation is not as simple as handing out free trees. But it really isn't all that tough, either. It's not only worthwhile, it's vital. Let's just do it correctly.

There's a popular bumper sticker on our highways and byways that reads, *Trees Are the Answer*. It should read, *Native Trees Are the Answer*.

11

❧

Amaze Your Neighbors: Have an Ecologically Sound Landscape

❧

Sally

How can I break this to you gently? If you're an average American homeowner, your present landscape is undoubtedly an ecological disaster. But—it doesn't have to stay that way.

The best way for you to start having an ecologically sound landscape is to radically change your ideas about gardening, especially those that concern soil and bugs. The post–World War II tradition of "rescue by chemical warfare" is now known to be more destructive than helpful. Today, hundreds of landscaping professionals are turning to nature to figure out ways to combat bugs and diseases and to grow healthier plants in an ecologically safe manner. After all, Mother Nature kept things going for millions of years, while we seem to have polluted our soil and water and air to an amazing extent in less than fifty. By studying and imitating nature, scientists are unearthing some interesting information and some novel approaches on how to garden.

The basis for all ecologically sound gardening is the soil. Healthy soil is not an inert substance; it is alive with millions of microorganisms. These microscopic plants and animals make nitrogen available to higher plants. They also move air and water through the soil. All of these activities are essential for healthy plant life. Commercial nitrogen fertilizers suppress these microbes until they become greatly reduced in number and are unable to function. Toxic pesticides, fungicides, and herbicides kill these important microbes outright.

Is your soil dead? If you are a traditional gardener who applies pre-emergents every spring and sprays every time you see an insect or a brown spot on your lawn, then your soil *is* probably dead. At the very least, it's in a deep coma.

But it can be brought back to life. The first step is to stop spraying poisons. The second is to stop using fertilizers high in nitrogen salts. The third step is to start rebuilding your soil the organic way.

Some organic experts recommend a "shotgun" approach in which you aerate the soil, add compost, and spray liquid seaweed or fish emulsion or mixtures of these and other substances on the leaves of your plants until the soil has healed itself. Aeration and compost are the two big steps because they will restore the microbes to the soil in abundant numbers. If you have no microbes to bring back to life, you can add them. I used to use compost starter with great results. Now there is a mycorrhizal product you can buy for sunny soils and a good fungal one for forest soils.

There are many ways to aerate soil, and compacted soils aren't the only kind that need it. If, for example, the soil has been chemically abused for years, it is badly in need of aeration. This can be done physically by tilling, by turning the soil with a pitchfork or by a mechanical aerifier that punches deep holes in the ground. (Do not, of course, do this within the dripline of a tree. Instead, see chapter 20, "Leave Those Leaves.")

After aerating the soil, dig in plenty of composted material. Soil with a high humus (compost) content absorbs rainwater readily and holds it longer than soil denuded of humus. Clay soils naturally retain humus more easily than sandy soils through which moisture runs very fast, leaching out the nutrients and minerals.

Any organic matter that is broken down to the consistency of potting soil is perfect. This can be compost you make yourself, sacks of composted cow manure, or truckloads of "dairy compost," as one supplier delicately calls it. Cow manure used to be very effective, but there are so many toxins present in cow feed these days (think what we're doing to corn), that probably you'd want to use certified organic manure only. Also, avoid composts made of cottonweed burs and other crops that are subjected to intense chemical attention.

Making your own compost is best. You can recycle all grass clippings, fallen leaves, and organic garbage in one compost pile, which takes from six months to a year to decompose. Heavier wood and brush obtained from pruning can be used in a brush pile. Brush takes two or more years to compost (it takes longer if your climate is on the dry side), but in the meantime, it makes a home for small reptiles like anoles and lizards and numerous helpful insects like spiders. (Maybe it's because *Charlotte's Web* made an early and strong impression on me, but it really sickens me to see how thoughtlessly we kill spiders for no other reason than that they are there. Be glad they are, and protect them.)

Getting back to composting—wait until you hear what they've done in Fredericksburg, Texas. Starting in the early seventies, residents have been raking their autumn leaves into piles near the curb. (No plastic bags!) The city then comes by and picks them up with a leaf-picker. The leaves are carted off to the sewage treatment plant and spread into two parallel rows that are closed off at the ends to make a narrow pond. Sludge is pumped in between the rows at intervals, and the piles are turned with a front-loader until everything has turned to compost. Residents then drive over in their pickup trucks and buy back their leaves—now as enriched compost—for $3 to $8 a cubic yard, considerably less than store-bought fertilizers.

Although this is not a money-making proposition for the city, there is a long-term advantage in cutting landfill costs. They are planning to expand the program to include grass clippings and brush. They are also planning to speed up the composting process. Relying on rainfall as they do now, the leaves take a year to compost. If watering is added to the process, the leaves could be composted by spring, in time to accommodate grass clippings which could be composted by fall. Is your community doing something like this? If not, dash off a note to your mayor.

How do you add in compost if you have established perennial flower or shrub beds? Take your cue from nature. What does nature do each year to renew the soil? The answer is mulch. It is rare to see bare soil in nature. In woodlands or forests, the soil is protected and renewed by a mulch of dead leaves. In prairies and meadows, a thatch of grass litter does the same thing. If you live in the desert, notice that your natural soil amendment is rocks (called desert pavement), not compost.

In traditional flower and vegetable gardens, landscaped beds were proudly kept weed-free so that only bare soil showed around the plants. It is now suspected that even weeds are ecologically preferable to exposed soil. Some experts recommend three to four inches of mulch, topped off all year. Some apply it once in the spring. If you live in an area that receives thirty inches or more of moisture a year, I recommend one to two inches of compost in late spring to protect the ground in the summer. In the fall, rake in fallen leaves; they'll decompose in early spring, after providing a comforter all winter.

Mulches do much more than add organic matter to the soil; they also aid in temperature control. Bare soil in the summer in full sunlight can bake at 122°F. With a mulch, your plants' roots can stay a comfortable 82° to 84°F.

Mulches also help retain water. The amount of evaporation of water from soil or through the leaves of plants can be immense. Estimates for west Texas and the Southwest deserts far exceed the annual rainfall averages. Stones can be an effective mulch in those arid areas where organic mulches are not feasible.

Once your soil is in good shape, insect damage is minimal. This is a hard connection for many people to understand. But sickly plants are more attractive to insects. It's like wolves preying on only the old or weaker members of the bison herd.

Once you stop spraying insecticides, you'll also have fewer insects that are harmful to your plants because you won't have killed their natural predators. Ladybugs, praying mantises, and spiders gobble up thousands of aphids every day. Unfortunately, these longer-lived, more specialized insects are far more vulnerable to poison than the spider mites and aphids you are trying to get rid of.

Birds are harmed when they eat poisoned insects, and so are bats. (Yes, I love bats, too! Now you know it all.) They're responsible for eating a zillion tons of mosquitoes each summer. There are actually *fewer* mosquitoes when bats eat them than there are if the bats are killed and man tries to control the mosquitoes with poisons.

In an unpoisoned, natural garden, there is a variety of insects but not too many of any one type. You'll have a good balance of bees and butterflies, ladybugs and caterpillars (which might become butterflies), pill bugs (which also make compost) and June bugs (to feed the mockingbirds), cicadas (so it *sounds* like a summer afternoon) and so on.

Another way to reduce insect damage is to install a greater variety of plants. If, for instance, you have an entire flowerbed planted in marigolds, spider mites will be attracted to the marigold feast. But, if you have only a few marigolds and thirty other kinds of perennials and annuals, no one kind of insect will be attracted.

Of course, in the process of converting your garden to an ecologically healthy one, before everything is in balance, you still might get a major aphid attack or be the convention center for a meeting of mites. If so, you can buy and release predator insects to clean up the pests for you.

In 1991, it cost David Hoover, a landscape contractor in Dallas, $2,500 to spray a conventional pesticide on a fifty-three-acre business complex he maintained that was infested with aphids. The operation had to be done at night when there was no wind and no people to harm from drifting spray. The result was a total failure. "In some areas," he observed, "the populations actually seemed to increase after spraying."

So he released 10,000 lacewing larvae. Within two weeks, the aphids seemed to be all gone. But then, after six weeks, they were beginning to reappear. Because the lacewings live only about three weeks, Hoover released two more batches of 500 lacewing larvae each at three-week intervals to help a reproducing population get going. Today, the problem seems to be well under control, although Hoover is prepared to continue occasional releases until the system is entirely self-supporting. His cost? Just $440.

Impressed, Hoover decided to test them in his home garden. He gently placed thirty lacewing larvae on a rose bush loaded with aphids. In less than two weeks, the aphids were gone and have not returned. Can you imagine how inexpensive and easy this method would be for your home landscape? And how clear your conscience would be?

Seriously, is there anything we've mentioned so far that seems beyond your abilities? We don't think so.

And now that you've resolved to convert your landscape into an ecologically sound example for all of your neighbors to ooh and ahh over, listen to this: Some folks are actually moving beyond just being ecologically sound and are imitating natural landscapes. Woodlands, prairies, and savannas—those edges where woods and grasslands meet—are being successfully mimicked in front and backyards all over the country. This extends the habitats of our shrinking wilderness areas and park systems, and provides a safe sanctuary for endangered wildlife that are losing their natural breeding and feeding sites.

~

Better Things
for Better Living
through ... Organic?

~

Andy

When you are involved with plants and landscaping—profession-ally or as a layperson—it's inevitable that sooner or later some-one will try to make you commit yourself on the "organic gardening versus chemicals" question. Sally's knee-jerk reaction used to be, "Well, of course, I'm all for organic gardening. Who wants nasty chemi-cals all over the yard?"

But then it dawned on her that she was going along with that old label-ing game, the way we often do in politics. Someone is labeled a liberal and a line is drawn. Someone else is labeled a conservative and we know exactly what to think about him or her. Only it's never that cut-and-dried.

So, what does it mean when someone says they're against chemicals? Chemicals are nothing more than compounds made out of elements. *We*

"Personally, I prefer my aphids with a tad less dursban."

are made up of chemicals, like DNA. And many chemicals—all those containing carbon atoms—are organic.

One day, as we were discussing this, Sally announced that what we're really talking about here is not chemicals versus organic—that's a meaningless comparison. We're talking toxic versus nontoxic.

Even that designation may be too simplistic. A lot of natural (organic) things are very toxic. You wouldn't want to eat oleander blossoms. Tapioca in its natural state is highly toxic; when we buy it as pudding mix, it's been heavily processed to make it safe. Arsenic is a deadly poison, but it's used by homeopathic physicians in a very diluted and purified form as a treatment for numerous ailments. And, of course, there's tobacco. . . .

Many "organic" pesticides that are supposed to target specific garden pests but not harm the "good" critters are destructive to the larvae of butterflies or the immature form of ladybugs.

So the question is not, do we want chemicals on our lawns and in our gardens? The question is, do we want poisonous substances in our landscapes that have far-reaching and harmful effects on us and our environment?

Sad to say, much of what we buy and use today is far from safe. Read what it says on those weed killer bottles (the operative word here is "killer"). Some of these products warn you not to let your pets or children play on the lawn for twenty-four hours after application, or until the stuff has dried. But you can usually smell the poisons for days. Is it really safe to walk barefoot or roll in the grass the next day?

The list of harmful effects from our continuing use of toxic over-the-counter garden products includes skin rash, chronic respiratory diseases, nausea, dizziness, damage to our endocrine and immune systems, reductions in male fertility, deformities in male genitalia, fetal damage, and cancer. There is also growing concern about how some lawn chemicals interact with prescription drugs. And there is plenty of evidence that children, with their smaller developing bodies, are more vulnerable to poisons than adults are.

A study reported in the *Journal of the National Cancer Institute* indicates a possible link between an increase in childhood leukemia and parents' use of certain common garden chemicals. Warren Porter, chair of the zoology departments at the University of Wisconsin, Madison, expresses concerns felt by many in the scientific community when he asks, "Do we value dandelion-free lawns over our children?"

According to Victor Kimm, formerly with the Environmental Protection Agency, "Many people haven't fully appreciated the inherently toxic nature of lawn-care products." I guess not, since the EPA estimates that we're dumping over 25 million pounds of herbicides and 30 million pounds of pesticides on residential lawns and gardens each year. And, 21 million homeowners are applying the stuff themselves without any real idea of what they are handling. Beyond Pesticides (formerly The National Coalition against the Misuse of Pesticides) claims the total for all uses, including industrial, commercial, and governmental settings, is 285 million pounds!

And something else: what the heck do you do with the empty containers or the bottles that are still half full? We've got several of them in our garage, holdovers from our unenlightened days. We know we just can't dump this stuff down the drain or in the gutter, but many people do. And we can't blithely consign them to the garbage can and, ultimately, the landfill, although that is also a common practice. Many communities have set up programs that will safely dispose of these poisons, but many have not, and most people don't even think to ask or take the trouble to use the service if it is available. And how safe is the safe disposal? We hope safer than our nuclear waste storage!

Water departments in various communities have started adding a surcharge to water bills. The money is supposed to pay for monitoring storm water runoff. When the Safe Drinking Water Act was passed two decades ago, the EPA thought our only worry was sewage. Now they know better. Runoff carrying toxic chemicals from lawns, as well as other pollutants, is a growing threat. This is one added charge we don't mind paying.

Public awareness is also changing, without which nothing else happens. The next time you think that your lawn and garden need a spritz of something to kill some insects or weeds, don't be so quick to grab the first bottle on the garden-center shelf. Think about what happens *after* the weed or the aphid is dead.

Remember that a healthy plant can usually fight off bugs and diseases on its own. Plant native or other well-adapted plants. Use mulches, beneficial soil organisms, or even water (in a drought) to strengthen the plant. Be patient: the natural predators might show up. Nearly every "problem" in our garden has solved itself without our taking any action at all.

And read. There are a number of good books on the subject of organic gardening. Also contact Beyond Pesticides at 701 E Street Southeast, Washington, DC 20003, or call them at 202-543-8314 for the latest on gardening chemicals.

Sally has a good rule of thumb—"Don't spray your garden with anything you wouldn't want sprayed on yourself."

PART III

Putting It All Together

As it is, whatever the circumstances,
I have always tried to shape gardens each
as a harmony, linking people to nature,
house to landscape, the plant to its soil.

—RUSSEL PAGE,
The Education of a Gardener

This used to be among my prayers—a piece
of land not so very large, which would contain a
garden, and near the house a spring of ever-flowing
water, and beyond these a bit of wood.

—HORACE

13

⁓

Requiem for a Lawnmower

⁓

Sally

Everyone has heard of Murphy's Law (Whatever can go wrong will go wrong), and the Peter Principle (People rise to their level of incompetence). Now I'd like to introduce you to Sally's Axiom: The more boring the front yard, the greater the need for upkeep and maintenance.

Picture the kind of yard I'm talking about: meticulously clipped hedges, all squared off and boxy; closely cropped golf course–quality lawns; regimental rows of begonias. And, of course, the obligatory trashy shade tree (Norway maple, Siberian elm, fruitless mulberry, Bradford pear . . .) probably stuck in by the builder and most likely ringed by an "inner tube" of impatiens. You see this pattern replicated in neighborhood after neighborhood, all over America.

Is this some sinister plot? How did our landscapes get to look like this?

Back when there was still plenty of wildland, a high-maintenance landscape—the obvious work of human hands and not Mother Nature—was a way of making people feel more in control of their lives and their environment.

After all, how would anyone know they'd just tamed the land if it didn't look markedly different? Even more important, people lived in mortal fear of what the neighbors would think of them if every weed and stray branch weren't instantly removed. In 1875, a guy named Peter Henderson wrote a book entitled *Gardening for Pleasure*. In it he made it quite clear what he thought of people who didn't conform to the well-manicured look: "It is gratifying to know that such neighbors are not numerous, for the example of the majority will soon shame them into decency."

Happily, the trend is reversing. People (and gardens) are loosening up. It's okay to spend your day off having fun instead of mowing, edging, and hedging. And now, instead of wildland threatening us, it desperately needs our help to survive. Small tracts that have escaped being developed are now being preserved as parks, much as endangered animals are preserved in zoos.

Do you look upon mowing your lawn as good physical exercise . . . the equivalent of a rousing set of tennis, or a three-kilometer jog? Or do you see it as a time for meditation, with the sound of the mower acting as a sort of mantra? Or is it expiation for your sins, along the lines of self-flagellation? No? Good, then you'll be glad to know that you can redesign your garden and hold a requiem for your lawnmower. Candles are optional.

It was way back in 1983 when Andy and I bade an untearful farewell to our old muscle-powered mower. We'd been working up to this wonderful event ever since we'd moved into our Dallas home a few years before. We lived on about an eighth of an acre, and our two-story house took up about a third of that space.

Here is the story of how we inexpensively converted our boring, ordinary front yard into a native, naturalistic garden that looked pretty all year, fed numerous birds, anoles, raccoons, opossums, fireflies, and a woodhouse toad, required no fertilizers, no insecticides, no herbicides, and almost no work at all.

When we moved in, we inherited a St. Augustine lawn fringed with a collection of standard (that is to say, nonnative) evergreen shrubs. About mid-June of the first summer in our home, I accepted the upkeep of the yard as my responsibility in the marriage. (Andy's was to keep a vigilant eye open for falling meteors.) To keep everything green, I had to set out the sprinkler every night in some part of the yard, moving it around on a rotating basis, and, even harder, remembering to turn it off again.

That first June water bill reinforced my feelings that this was not the right way to go, and mowing that lawn was going to be a sweaty chore. Besides, being a sensitive and enlightened kinda guy, Andy hated to watch me pushing that mower under the broiling Texas sun. I suggested we find a different approach.

My response was to quit watering. Well, almost. Dallas is set on rich black prairie clay with a shrink-swell factor that is murderous on foundations. I wasn't so dumb that I quit watering the foundation. But I did cut back to about one soaking a month from June through September when daytime temperatures were often over 100°F and some nights never cooled below 90°F.

By September it was very evident that many shrubs and trees were not going to survive on this regimen, so I cut to the ground everything that was too wimpy and ill adapted. By the end of the next summer, more shrubs had eliminated themselves from the landscape.

The next fall, following the epiphany I described in my Introduction, I took a course on landscaping with native plants. My homework assignment was to draw a native landscape plan for our house. I liked my front yard flower garden design so much that I decided to actually execute it. (Andy says, "Notice who makes the decisions in this family." I reply, "Notice who does all the work!")

Because at that time I was still new to this landscape design business, I started small, experimenting with an area ten feet by ten feet, down by the street. When that became established, I moved on to another patch. And so on until the entire St. Augustine lawn was gone, replaced by a profusion of Turk's cap, inland seaoats, zexmenia, pavonia, spiderwort, ruellia, meadowrue, and other savanna flowers. Many of the original plant materials came from my usual practice of scrounging wildflowers from vacant lots. I also ordered whatever native flowers and seeds were available from commercial sources. The ones that had been collected in my own state did infinitely better than those from out of state.

To facilitate getting around in the garden, I designed a gently winding limestone path from the street up to the front steps and another one cutting across from the neighbor's yard so the mailman wouldn't tread on our wildflowers. And, because the flagstones were really big, I hired some young guys with strong backs to install them. This was the only outside labor involved.

When the last blade of turf grass was gone, we set the lawnmower on the curb. It was gone within the hour.

Starting small has several advantages: it's easier on the back and the wallet. And, as Andy points out, it also allows you to sneak up on the neighbors. If I'd converted the entire front yard to a naturalistic style all at once, our very conservative neighbors might have freaked out. But by taking it a section at a time, it allowed them to get used to what we were doing.

For years, the shady area to the left of our driveway had been eager to return to a ground carpet of native violets. The lady from whom we'd bought the house apologized to us for them. She assured us that she had done the best she could by carefully poisoning them every year. I'm happy to tell you that after we moved in, they made a grand comeback.

Each fall, a wonderful thing happened. Leaves fell off the trees and we allowed them to remain on the ground to form a winter blanket that was mostly decomposed by early spring. I soon noticed that the clay soil was getting soft and was pleasant to dig in. It was no longer like hacking into concrete! And earthworms were numerous—a sure sign that we had healthy soil.

And that's the way things stayed until we moved some fifteen years later. We lived happily with this landscape, and apparently the neighbors liked it, too. A jogger would come by regularly; one day he told Andy that he liked coming down our street just to see what was in bloom that week. And on more than one occasion people would drive up, get out of their cars carrying cameras and ask us if they could pose their kids in our wildflowers.

Maintenance? Remember Sally's Axiom? People assume that a naturalistic landscape consisting of over forty different species would require *more* upkeep, not less. The truth is, our maintenance consisted of maybe twelve hours all year: deadheading, some judicious pruning, and a little weeding—about three days' worth a year, twice in the spring and once again after frost. Every other year I'd pay to get the trees trimmed.

Because we weren't spending inordinate amounts of time doing maintenance, we were free to simply enjoy our garden. We sat in it, we ate in it, our cats played in it, and our daughter and her friends grew up getting acquainted with a wonderful natural world of butterflies and birds and lizards and other critters. And, yes, we also admit that there were times when we couldn't help but feel a little smug as we watched our neighbors out mowing their lawns.

❧

Landscape Design for Geeks and Nerds

❧

Sally

How's this for a sweeping generality?—CPAs, math professors, NASA rocket scientists, and bowlers who can compute their own scores should not design landscapes.

I thought of this recently as I was driving down an interstate that had been landscaped by the highway department. The trees were all lined up with mathematical precision. Mother Nature would never have done that—that took an engineering mentality.

Frankly, there are people who should not even think about designing their own gardens. Good intentions alone won't cut it—just like wanting to sing an aria doesn't guarantee that you'll make it through *Ah, fuggi il traditor* without hitting a clinker.

The fact is, a sense of design is not learned; you're either born with it or you aren't. The best landscape designers I know are artists. And, even though their training leans heavily toward engineering, the best landscape architects I know also have artistic souls. If you're good at arranging a room so that it looks inviting or if you take vacation photos that your friends actually look forward to seeing, you can probably design an attractive landscape. If you also have trouble balancing your checkbook and never really got the hang of the seven-times table, then an attractive landscape design is pretty much guaranteed.

Just remember, when you step into the field of landscape design, you are working on a larger scale than usual. Don't be intimidated by the size of your canvas.

As for the rest of you—the ones who admit to having little or no artistic sense—well, you're probably *still* going to tackle a garden design at some point, aren't you? In that case, let me give you a few pointers.

For the front landscape, make your house the focus of the overall design; your eye should immediately be attracted to the front entrance. If you live on a corner lot, you need to wrap the design around to include the side yard. It should all flow together smoothly, not be chopped up into disjointed units.

Elements such as the driveway, front walk, grass, and beds need to be in scale with the home. If the house is large and generous, your garden should be as well. Two-story houses need taller trees than ranch-style houses. Stand across the street to visualize the right proportions for your house. Look at your imaginary design from down the street as though you were arriving in a car.

In the backyard, the focus is usually the sitting area, which can be lawn, terrace, patio, deck, gazebo, or pool. This is also the main point of view, even though the view out of the back windows is also very important. If this doesn't make sense to you, and you can't visualize a landscape design that gets you excited, go back and read the third paragraph again. Then, call in a professional designer or a talented friend to help you with this part of your plan—preferably one who needs all of his or her fingers to give you a cost estimate.

Design aside, choosing the plants, planting them, keeping them alive, and maintaining them properly is well within the abilities of *everyone.* You just have to think, trust your own observations, and not believe everything you're told. Rigid ideas about when to prune, how to plant, and what products to use are sometimes hard-won knowledge, but sometimes they are also old wives' tales. Orthodoxies also have a habit of changing every few years. I've found that patient observation of natural landscapes and good common sense are the most important qualities for successful garden design.

But, you ask, can't I get all of the information I need at my local nursery? Well, yes and no. Obviously, there are many experienced nursery people who can be founts of useful information. But, during what time of the year are you most likely to visit the nursery? Probably, in the spring and summer, when they are busiest and have taken on a gaggle of college students to help out. These helpers are often eager and willing but woefully ignorant, I'm afraid, and you're likely to go away with some bad advice. You'd be amazed at some of the misinformation I've received over the years from sincere, well-meaning part-time help.

And, unless they have a well-established demonstration garden, a nursery is not the best place to find out what your plant will eventually look like. Nursery stock is grown in an artificial environment of fake soil, heat unnatural to the season, regular fertilization and water, and overcrowding. This practice is necessary to produce beautiful plants in a short time in a small space. It's the only way plants can be grown at a price you can afford and also allow the nursery to stay in business. But any plant from any climate and soil can be grown in this artificial environment. Just because a plant looks good at your local nursery does not mean that it will be right when faced with the realities of life in your garden.

Besides, nursery plants tend to be what you'd expect in a nursery: babies. You need to know how large they will become. Many people unknowingly place huge shrubs inches from a sidewalk and then have to skootch around it in later years to get to the front door. Often trees that can reach fifty feet and will get twenty-four-inch trunks are planted under the eaves of the house. Just because a shrub comes in a one-gallon container doesn't mean it won't grow up to be a twenty-five-foot tree.

If you keep the eventual size in mind, you won't make mistakes like crowding large shrubs too closely together. And, you won't kill off sun-loving plants that wind up in the shade of another plant that you didn't realize would grow so tall.

The most important choices for your landscape are trees. They are the tallest elements in your design, and you want trees that are long-lived so that your garden will steadily improve with age. You also want them to be healthy and that means that they must be able to withstand all the extremes of hot, cold, flood, and drought that your area can produce. They also have to really like the soil you have, because tree roots can cover as much as 10,000 square feet. I've known a lot of people who try, but you can't really change the geology of your property.

To meet all of these requirements, you will find that the vast majority (usually over 90 percent) of your choices will be trees native to your property. And, if you live on a hilltop, the trees in the nearest creek bottom are not native for *you*. To find out which trees are really adapted to your site, you'll need to observe the nearest forested *hilltop*.

If you don't know how to recognize one tree from another, take along a guidebook. Choose a regional one, if at all possible. It is easy to get really far off track with a guide that was written for a national market. Or, take approximately one foot off the tip of a branch and carry it to a nature center or the local college's botany department for identification.

While you're still at the location that approximates your home site, observe what shrubs and grasses and flowers are there, and identify them the same way. One big key to a successful design is to group your plants by water needs. The plants growing beside an appropriate tree for your garden are likely to be appropriate also. (If you like them. Never force yourself to have a plant you don't like.)

Notice which ones grow right under trees and which ones grow in full sun, which ones grow only in swales and which ones grow only on slopes, which ones seem to sucker and which ones are politely self-contained. From an aesthetic point of view, observe which colors are especially pretty together, how the textures of certain leaves or tree trunks leap into prominence, and which forms are upright and which are spreading.

It is time to head for the nursery only when you have made up a plant list of usable species. If the plants you want are not in stock, talk to the nursery owner. If he knows he has a sure sale, he should be happy to order them from a commercial grower.

Once the design is laid out and the plants are chosen and purchased, you need to get the plants happily established in their new home. This is where common sense is of paramount importance.

Watering is difficult, like feeding a newborn baby. Plants, like babies, don't adhere to a strict schedule. When they're thirsty, they want attention *right away*! Some soils hold moisture for a long time and others dry quickly. Some plants prefer to grow roots in very moist soils that would make others rot. Some plants have leaves that droop dramatically when they are thirsty and give you only two or three days to rescue them. Others are stoic and look fine until they suddenly turn crispy, and then it's too late.

Soak the area around the plant thoroughly right after planting. Check the soil dampness with your finger frequently for the first couple of weeks and regularly through the first summer. For trees and large shrubs, check through the second summer, too. Even during the cooler parts of the year, be sure to water if you go for a couple of months without rain.

Then, after your plants are established and growing well, all except your bedding flowers and vegetables should be able to do without watering at all—unless you hit a very bad drought that goes on for several years. No matter where you live, an inch of water once a month is the most you should ever have to water to keep your garden looking optimal.

Let's also remember pruning and mowing—both are vital to the good looks of a landscape, though these are aesthetic judgments. But once the basic look and timing are established, these chores can be done by anyone—even left-brainers.

I hope I haven't made the creation of a landscape sound too complicated. It really isn't all that tough. In fact, it's as easy as two plus two equals . . . uh. . . .

❦

Made for the Shade

❦

Sally

The expression "made in the shade" connotes incredible ease and an absence of effort involved in some undertaking. Right! Tell that to a gardener who has labored unsuccessfully for years, trying to keep some flora alive in the dark shadows of a giant tree or along the northern side of a wall.

These shade gardeners are numerous. I know, because the question I get asked most often, and usually with a note of desperation, has to do with what will survive—never mind thrive—in full or partial shade. The inquirer is usually someone who has seen countless plants succumb in a sunless location and is almost ready to assign that portion of the property to horseshoe pitching.

To figure out what will work for you, we first need to talk about the three different types of shade we encounter. Plants that thrive in dappled or partial shade might dwindle and die in the absolute shade found on the north side of a two-story building. No flower I am aware of can do well in that situation.

Total shade can be found under a low-growing, very dense evergreen such as a magnolia or a blue spruce, where the sun never reaches. Don't waste your time here. In nature, all you'll find is a mulch of needles or dry leaves. In your home landscape, leaves or needles are quite acceptable. Or, you can use a mulch of pecan hulls or pea gravel or trim the tree up seven feet and install a patio or deck. Use flagstone or brick set in sand. It is vital that air and water be able to reach the roots of the tree.

Dappled shade is what you typically find under a deciduous tree such as a maple, oak, sweetgum, or tulip poplar. There is sun all day long, but it is filtered by leaves and reaches the ground only in shifting patches. This is a fun area to work in. If you have a fairly large area, at least fifteen feet by twenty feet, you can combine understory trees and groundcovers to create a miniature woodland that requires maintenance only once a year and attracts nesting pairs of birds.

For very early spring, plant small pink or white blooming understory trees such as redbud, amelanchier, or various kinds of native hawthorns. Underneath them plant wild violets and other woodland flowers that also blossom at this time. Blue phlox, pink trillium, golden groundsel, and white foamflower are some eastern flowers that carpet forest floors.

After the trees have leafed out, the beauty of a woodland comes mostly from the many shades and textures of green. It is important to have understory trees and shrubs and knee-high groundcovers to give enough interest in heights. Combine plants that have large leaves with those that have very small leaves, shiny leaves with finely cut leaves like those found on ferns or meadow rue, or leaves with white undersides and leaves with red stems. Choose plants that will have clusters or different sizes of ripening fruits.

Small evergreen trees or large shrubs are important for winter beauty and for privacy screening. Using evergreens that are native to your area, as opposed to those from Japan or northern Europe, usually has many advantages. The biggest bonus is not having to water them—unless you're in a long-term drought. They will be much healthier and unlikely to succumb to a freak freeze.

If a flower garden, not an easy-care woodland, is your heart's desire in a spot of dappled shade, there are a number of flowers that bloom well in bright dappled shade all day. Your flower garden will not be as dense and colorful as an English perennial border, but you can have an enjoyable rhythm of delicate textures and scattered color.

For spring, choose columbines or a local woodland phlox. The red or yellow columbines are better than the Colorado blue ones and much better than the McKana hybrids if you live where summers are hot. Phloxes are usually lavender, with some pink, some blue, and some white.

For summer, if you live in the Deep South choose Turk's cap and scarlet sage—both red. Far north, or up in the Appalachian mountains where summers are cool, this is the main blooming season and there are lots of choices. Goatsbeard, black cohosh, bowman's root, or other white woodland species can give dramatic accents.

Fall brings cardinal flowers, purple to lavender woodland asters, bright yellow woodland goldenrods, and lots of yellow daisies that consent to struggle in dim light.

Partial shade is usually a little sunnier than dappled shade. It is defined as full sun for part of the day and full or dappled shade for the rest of the day. If you're getting full sun in the morning, use the same plants you'd use for dappled shade, and you'll find that they will grow a little more densely and bloom more profusely.

However, if you're getting full sun in the afternoon, when temperatures are at their peak and the direct sun lasts four to five hours, you have a choice of a number of savanna flowers, shrubs, and small trees that can tolerate both full sun and partial shade. They might bloom a little less showily than in full sun, but the bloom time is extended and less water is needed to maintain their fresh appearance.

Viburnums give flowers in May and colored foliage in the fall. American beautyberry, coralberry, and snowberry are shrubs that have purple or white berries in the fall and often into winter. For perennials, several of the following are probably native to your area or will adapt to a flowerbed: black-eyed Susan, purple coneflower, bergamot, ruellia, spiderwort, veronica, and coreopsis.

Finding our own native understory trees and shrubs in nurseries is harder than finding Asian ones. Locating native flowers is much more difficult than finding begonias, caladiums, and impatiens, but the search is well worth the effort. Once you have experienced a shady native garden, rich in a variety of colors and textures, different at every season, fragrant with sweet and spicy scents, and alive with songbirds and butterflies, the contemporary American garden consisting of only one to three species seems incredibly boring.

~

How to Keep from Killing Your Wooded Lot

~

Sally

When Ed and Gigi saw the wooded lot, it was love at first sight. They bought the property and immediately began to plan their dream home. They didn't know that within the year, much of the natural beauty of their lot would disappear.

There was a delightful cluster of small trees in front that created a feeling of woodland right where the front door would be. These small trees were actually large by nursery standards; the trunks were four to eight inches in diameter. Best of all, in the back were three majestic, 200-year-old post oaks. These oaks would be the centerpiece of their backyard landscape, which included a creek on the rear property line.

Ed and Gigi noticed that the entire development that they were moving into, although brand new, still retained many mature trees. Clearly this was an enlightened developer; he had made a sincere effort to preserve the natural beauty of the land. Like a growing number of developers today, he seemed sensitive to conservation, if only for a dollars-and-cents reason;

this developer realized that trees are an asset to a property, increasing both its visual and sales value.

We still run across builders who bulldoze every trace of vegetation, level the terrain in all directions, and then magnanimously stick a few five-gallon trash trees in the front yard.

Ed and Gigi bought their lot in late spring. By November their house was built and they moved in, amid a swirl of autumn leaves. Thanks to the developer, the venerable oaks out back were preserved in a cradle of railroad ties that formed a series of terraces down the steep bank to the creek. The miniwoods in front had been attractively landscaped with shrubs, and sod had been laid. All seemed well.

When spring arrived, the three large oaks remained virtually bare. One was clearly dead, one was covered with white mildew and very likely dead, and the third oak was struggling to survive.

Was some virulent disease doing the damage?

The problem is a common one, simply a case of good intentions gone awry. The developer had unwittingly done a lot of things wrong.

First mistake: Soil was piled up around the base of the tree trunks. This excess soil held moisture against the trunks, instead of allowing it to seep down to the roots. Mildew developed and began creeping upward, rotting the bark. Even worse, this extra soil was suffocating the trees. Most trees breathe through roots that are close to the surface, where oxygen is present in the soil. A tree's trunk should flare out slightly at ground level. If no flare is visible, soil has been piled up too high; even three extra inches of dirt can seriously harm a tree. On Ed and Gigi's lot, the flares were buried under twelve to eighteen inches of dirt.

Second mistake: Workers inadvertently hacked away at the trunks, usually by running into them with bulldozers and by piling lumber, bricks, and trash up against them. Patches of bare, exposed wood were the result, which interrupted the natural flow of sap—the tree's bloodstream. When this happens, the branches overhead die. If a tree has bark missing on more than one side, it is almost surely doomed. The surviving tree, at this writing, is hanging on only because it had the least amount of damage inflicted on its bark.

Third mistake: More than one-half the roots had been chopped off to make room for the house, the concrete-slab patio, and the railroad-tie terracing. A tree's roots extend out one and one-half times as far as the branches overhead. Destruction of the roots results in a corresponding dieback of the branches.

Ed and Gigi's loss could easily have been avoided if they (and their builder) had been aware of these facts. But, knowing the facts is not always enough.

A few years back our friend, Ron, lived through a landscaping nightmare. He had purchased a lushly wooded lot and planned to build his home there. Ron is an architect, and he knows how to preserve trees. Still, he couldn't have foreseen what eventually happened.

The trouble began because another home was being built on the adjoining lot. One day, Ron discovered that the neighbor's bulldozer had run amok on his property and destroyed a large percentage of his mature trees. Of course Ron collected damages, but let's face it, no amount of money can replace a thirty-year-old woods. Not in less than thirty years, that is.

But the horror story did not end there. When it came time for Ron to build his own house, he gave specific instructions to *his* bulldozer operator. He marked off the trees that were to be saved with orange plastic ribbon and took time off from work to stand around and supervise. Trouble was, the bulldozer operator got back from lunch before Ron did. In less than fifteen minutes, six perfectly healthy, mature trees had been leveled. (To paraphrase P. J. O'Rourke, giving a bulldozer to some guys is like giving liquor and car keys to teenaged boys.)

Ron's home was to have been surrounded by woods. He wanted no lawn to mow, no groundcover to weed, and nothing to water. Mother Nature had already provided American elms, cedar elms, bois d'arcs, and junipers in abundance. Underneath were numerous understory trees, shrubs, and groundcovers—many of them evergreen. This natural wooded landscape, besides being beautiful, would have provided privacy, shade (which would have reduced his air-conditioning bills), erosion control, noise buffering from the nearby highway, and wonderful birdwatching.

Do you think these two stories are isolated incidents? If only that were true. These things happen all too often on individual lots, as well as on large tract developments. Here are some steps you can take to protect the existing trees on your land:

Assess all of the trees on your property. There are many good tree-identification books out on the market today, so stop by your local library or bookstore. If you feel incapable of identifying all of the trees yourself, ask a competent landscaper or arborist to visit your property for a consultation. But take care—don't get caught up in your consultant's personal prejudices. People often have very strong likes and dislikes of trees for very strange reasons. Don't accept at face value anyone's assessment of a tree as "trashy." Ask them why they feel that way. Get all the facts. And, remember that a tree you would never buy is often absolutely invaluable to your landscape if the tree is the right size and in the right place. I personally dislike hackberries, but I would have wept if I'd lost the huge one that shaded half of our home in Dallas.

Pay special attention to the smaller understory trees: viburnum, redbud, hawthorn, hollies, and so on. You'll probably find an abundance of them on your property. These trees are crucial to the maintenance of a true woodland look, and they provide gorgeous spring and fall color. They are also very important as nesting and feeding locales for wildlife. These understory trees, however, are usually cleared away, even by developers who make an effort to save the big stuff.

Thicket shrubs such as roughleaf dogwood or its relatives and smooth sumac should also be saved; they are useful for privacy, rounding out corners, and providing cover for birds.

The list will vary, depending on where you live, but you're also sure to find a treasury of native groundcovers and wildflowers: Virginia creeper, coralberry, coral honeysuckle, crossvine, wild asters, frostweed, violets, wild orchids, and fragrant phlox are the most frequent ones in the Dallas-Fort Worth area. Have fun finding them, but watch out for and remove poison ivy and greenbriar.

Plan where your house and driveway will go *only after* you've identified your trees and have selected the ones you most want to save. A good architect can be very clever in thinking of ways to keep all of your trees and have your house, too.

Wherever possible, barricade the trees out as far as their driplines. *Dripline* is the term used to describe the area on the ground directly beneath the furthest reach of the branches. This is usually where the roots are most active. Cutting the roots, burying them, or dumping building wastes such as cement or leftover paint on them is severely harmful.

Use snow fencing or build barriers of scrap lumber and tie bright Day-Glo plastic ribbon prominently on the barriers. This will not only help protect the trees, but it will keep the valuable understory and groundcovers intact. Sound expensive? Price a few large trees and you'll find that protecting what you've got is really the most economical option.

Arrange to be on the property *whenever* the bulldozer is in operation. Don't trust verbal or written instructions. (Take short lunches!)

Oversee the grading; don't let soil get piled up on the roots, and don't let poor drainage areas develop. Standing water can suffocate a tree even more quickly than extra soil. Following the natural lines of drainage is the best choice. Also, check neighboring lots to see how they might be channeling water your way.

Make an agreement with your builder that he or she will compensate you at a fixed amount for any injured tree. Make sure your builder knows that dumping building materials on roots is just as damaging as scraping the trunk and breaking branches.

After your house is finished and the workmen are gone, remove protective barriers. This is also the time to have your trees pruned. Choose someone for the job carefully. A good tree pruner is an artist who sees a tree as a sculpture; he or she would *never* cut off the end of a branch. Good pruning cleans out the middle of the tree and cuts branches off nearly flush with the main branch or trunk.

If you have a natural, wooded property, you are indeed fortunate. Protect it. Care for it. It will pay you back with great beauty and enjoyment for many decades.

~

Don't Let Your Wildflowers Run Wild

~

Sally

Wildflowers look so gorgeous growing along our roadsides that many people are fooled into thinking that they can grow wild-flowers successfully—and effortlessly—on their own properties. When they try, they learn that growing wildflowers and native grasses from scratch is often unexpectedly hard work.

Sometimes hundreds of dollars of seed and a lot of physical effort result in a waist-high weed patch. A weed patch is exactly what some of my former clients wound up with. They wanted a low-maintenance, naturally beautiful country landscape in their front yard. They envisioned native shrubs and trees close to the house and along a fence, and a buffalograss meadow, thick with wildflowers, stretching out to the road.

Their lot was situated between two other homes, each one having a beautiful wildflower meadow. Naturally, they thought having their own meadow would be easy.

In the fall, they hydromulched with buffalograss and a wildflower-seed mix. The results the following spring were definitely not spectacular. So, they immediately planted more wildflower seed. They repeated the process the next fall, and still again the next fall. After three and one-half years, they were thoroughly discouraged. The front yard was full of weeds.

Of the pounds and pounds of wildflower seed they had sown, only five individual flowers could be found that were of the species that had been deliberately planted. And, a fair stand of sun-loving buffalograss was being shaded out by tall weeds.

What went wrong?

First, they made the mistake of having the land bulldozed and reshaped. Bulldozing stirred up a lot of dormant weed seeds—junk stuff, trash—and destroyed the wildflowers they wanted. Ironically, they already had a flowery meadow. All they needed to do was to start meadow maintenance—no mowing during the growing season and one mow after frost. They could have pulled a few weeds, added a few more native species, and had their dream with very little effort.

Once the land was disturbed and they *had* to reseed, they compounded their first mistake by using an inappropriate seed mix—commonly called "meadow-in-a-can." While the mix they bought was from a company in their state, it was not a mix of flowers native to that state; it contained wildflowers from all over the world. This is not an uncommon problem with many commercial mixes.

A recent study of nineteen commercial wildflower seed mixes conducted at the University of Washington determined that each contained from three to thirteen invasive species and eight had seeds for plants that were considered noxious weeds in at least one U.S. state or Canadian province. Moreover, a third of the mixes had no content listing and another third provided inaccurate listings.

My clients could have collected seed from their neighbors' wildflowers and planted them. (All of the wildflowers they eventually ended up with came from right next door.) Or, they could have purchased *specific* wildflower seeds, once they'd determined which wildflowers were indigenous to their area. True, this takes some time and research, but the benefits make the effort worthwhile.

Finally, they didn't weed. They were trying for easy, remember? Well, there's no getting around it: You have to get out there and pull those weeds. And, you have to do it regularly for the first two years to allow the wildflowers to get established. The trick is to eliminate the weeds and *not*

the wildflower rosettes. (Two books on how to recognize rosettes are listed
in chapter 18, "To the Rescue!")

   Weeding doesn't have to be total misery. My advice is to put on a comfortable sunhat, take a jug of iced tea and a portable radio outside with you,
and just imagine that some wonderful benefactor is going to give you a
thousand dollars for every weed you yank.

Reliable Seed Sources

We were reluctant to add the following list, not because we don't have faith
in these companies, but because in the past when we put resource lists in
our books, the lists become obsolete in a year or two. Phone numbers and
addresses change, and companies go of business. The ones listed here are
either companies we've dealt with directly, or ones that have been recommended by trusted friends. This is by no means intended to be a comprehensive list, just a scattershot representation to give you some idea of who
is out there.

> **Blazing Star Wildflower Seed Company**, Saskatchewan, Canada,
>   306-289-2046 (tel and fax)
> **Ernst Conservation Seeds**, Meadville, Pennsylvania, www.ernstseed.com
> **Larner Seeds**, Bolinas, California, Info@larnerseeds.com
> **Native American Seed**, Junction, Texas, www.seedsource.com
> **Prairie Moon Nursery**, Winona, Minnesota, Pmnrsy@luminet.net
> **Prairie Nursery**, Westfield, Wisconsin, www.prairienursery.com
> **Plants of the Southwest**, Albuquerque and Santa Fe, New Mexico,
>   www.plantsofthesouthwest.com
> **Western Native Seed Company**, Coaldale, Colorado, Westseed@
>   chafee.net

To the Rescue!

❧

Sally

As a general rule, I don't approve of digging plants in the wild and bringing them into your home garden. We're trying to save natural habitats, not dismantle them. Never dig up plants on public lands. Never dig plants on private property without permission from the landowner. This is no joke—plant rustling can land you in jail.

However, there are times and circumstances when transplanting is not only okay but in fact desirable. I'm thinking specifically of organizations such as The Wild Ones or our friend Jeane Reeves of the Georgia Native Plant Society who conduct plant rescues. When they hear of natural land that is going to be destroyed to make way for a new housing development or shopping center, they organize volunteers to dig up and find safe homes for as many native plants as possible. Sometimes the plants go to private individuals and sometimes they go to schools, churches, or other public landscapes.

Another example of environmentally sound transplanting is when someone owns a tract of natural land and builds a home on it. They want to save as much of the native flora as possible, so they move small trees and shrubs from the "footprint" of the house and transplant them to another place on the property—often in close proximity to the finished house. This involves keeping these plants alive for a time by placing them on drip irrigation in a holding area.

Timing

Unfortunately, plant rescues can't always be done at the ideal time in the ideal way. The tips below are for what works best, if you do have a choice.

Some people think that transplanting is only a warm weather activity. This is true in the north where the ground freezes; you can't plant in frozen ground. However, in the south the best time of the year for planting is late fall to early winter. The reason is simple: a plant that is dug out of the ground loses 80 percent or more of its root system. It needs all winter to grow new roots before it must face the stress of flowering, fruiting, and leafing out, and before it has to contend with summer heat and drought.

Most people don't realize how extensive root systems are. A ten-foot-tall oak tree with a trunk three to four inches in diameter and branches ten feet wide has a dense root network extending fifteen to thirty feet across. But, after the tree is dug up, its root ball will typically be only two to three feet in diameter. That's an enormous loss and a great shock to the tree.

That's why you should pamper a transplanted tree with frequent watering for the first two to five years. The larger the tree, the higher the percentage of root loss. This means that a large tree needs more years to regrow its root system than does a small tree. Until the original roots are replaced, the tree will not put on new growth. A tree with a one-inch trunk often outgrows a four-inch tree within five years of each being transplanted. Flowers and grasses are much easier to transplant. Because they are smaller, they can usually regenerate their roots in one growing season.

The optimum time to transplant anything is on a misty or drizzling day in autumn. (Optimum for the plants, that is, not necessarily for you.) In high humidity, the tiny hair roots are less likely to dry out and be damaged, and your plant can start transporting moisture and growing new roots almost immediately.

Speed is also important. The faster you can get the plant back into the ground, the better it will fare.

Water the plant thoroughly after transplanting. This not only insures that plenty of moisture is available, but is also the gentlest way to melt the soil around the roots again so that no air pockets remain; air pockets dry out the roots.

Choosing Which Plants to Rescue

If at all possible, choose a new home for the plants that closely resembles their original home. Something from a rocky, dry area is not likely to grow well in moist garden loam.

You probably won't have the time or manpower to move every plant in need of rescue. Choose those with the best chance of survival. A plant that is young and small can be transplanted with more of its root system intact. I've learned from sad experience that when I move a nice big plant, a medium-sized one, and a small one, it's the small one that grows fastest and blooms first; the big one rarely survives.

Flowers and Grasses

Although flowers and grasses are relatively easy to transplant, there are basic rules to follow:

If the plant is an annual that goes from seed to flower and then dies all in one year, or a biennial that blooms the second year and dies, you will have better luck if you collect and plant seed rather than transplant. However, annuals and biennials can be transplanted in the fall in their rosette state.

Perennials also transplant best in their rosette state. A *rosette* is a sunburst of leaves that hugs the ground. A two- to five-inch rosette has a high rate of success. If you have several months' warning, you can identify the plants when they are in bloom, and mark the stems with plastic flagging tape. In fall, an experienced native plant person can identify the plants from their seed. Although fall is ideal for transplanting perennials, early spring before the flowering stem thrusts up will also work. You can find good pictures of rosettes in *Restoring Canada's Native Prairies* by John P. Morgan et al., and in *Parks' Success with Seeds* by Ann Reilly.

If a very old rosette is too big to move, dig out the small rosettes. The newest, most vigorous growth is always on the outer edges.

The most desirable grasses are perennials and they can be treated just like perennial flowers. They do not, however, have rosettes. The leaves turn brown and the plant goes dormant in the winter. Again, the vigorous new growth is on the outer edges of the mother plant. Remember to dig both outward and deeply to get plenty of roots. Of course on a plant rescue you might as well take the whole thing, after which you can divide it into smaller sections. If this is not a rescue, use surrounding soil to fill in the hole around the exposed roots of the mother plant so it will not suffer any permanent damage.

Trees and Shrubs

Trees that transplant best are found at least thirty feet away from competing trees and roots. If the trunk is one to eight inches in caliper (the diameter at chest level), you will have the best rate of success. For each inch of trunk diameter, you need to allow for nine to ten inches of root ball diameter. Plan ahead and be aware of how many strong friends you can count on. A tree that is three to four inches in caliper must have a root ball of at least thirty to forty inches in diameter. A root ball that size requires three average-sized men (or two hunks) to lift it out of the ground.

Make sure that the tree is in digable soil. Sandy soil is difficult because the root ball falls apart; be prepared to use plenty of burlap and wire. Rocky soil is fine for a one-inch caliper tree, unless the soil is too rocky to dig. Tight clay soil works best.

But, before you dig up that tree, go back and prepare its new home—the *receiving hole*. Make it shallow and very wide, and keep the sides of the hole rough, not hard-packed and smooth. Many plant people believe that hard-packed sides tend to trap the roots, as if they were in a pot, and prevent them from spreading out. Save the dirt for backfilling later. Fill the hole with water to make sure it will drain quickly; you should be able to see the water level sinking as you watch.

Only after you are sure that the receiving hole is ready should you dig up the tree. If the soil is too dry, the root ball will fall apart; come back a few days after a rain, or, if possible, water your tree deeply around the tree base and allow three days for the soil to dry to the right consistency of tacky-moist. If the ground is too wet, the root ball will also fall apart. (That's right, it's not as simple as you may have thought; now you know why nursery trees cost so much.)

Measure the width of the root ball and, with a clean, sharpened shovel, dig down around the perimeter, cutting cleanly through the roots. End at a point eighteen to twenty-seven inches underneath the trunk; that's where you can locate the tap root (if there *is* one). The finished root ball should be cone-shaped.

To hold the root ball firmly and disturb it as little as possible, wrap it with burlap and wire or, better, strong biodegradable rope. If the tree is only one inch in diameter, burlap and string is all you will need. Do not use synthetic burlap because it doesn't biodegrade and the roots won't be able to get out.

Once the root ball is firmly bound, make a sling or cradle to lift it out of the hole. Never lift the root ball out by the trunk. The weight of the soil is enough to tear the roots. From the sling, gently place the tree on a dolly or in a wheelbarrow. Cushion the trunk with burlap or old rags to prevent rubbing against metal or anything else that might injure the bark. If you transport a tree in a truck and the tree is in leaf, you must wrap the leaves to prevent dehydration.

Place the tree in the receiving hole, making sure that it is neither set in too high nor too low. Its original soil level should be exactly even with the new soil level. Otherwise, the roots will be either too far underground to breathe properly and the tree could literally suffocate, or too exposed and it will dry out. If you dug the receiving hole too deep, raise the level with original soil and tamp it firmly at the bottom of the hole. If the bottom of the hole is not packed hard, it could sink and your tree could sink with it. Even an inch or two can make a significant difference.

Backfill with the original soil. Don't fill in with compost or peat moss, thinking that you are doing the tree a favor. A little compost is fine, but as the tree consumes the compost, a vacuum is formed and the tree sinks to a dangerous level. A better way to get extra nutrients to the roots right after transplanting is to top dress with compost and slow-release organic fertilizers. Natural root stimulators are also helpful.

Correct watering is probably the most important aspect of getting your tree established. Many botanists believe that the air and water balance in the soil is the single most crucial factor in the health and growth of trees. Roots grow only as deep as the air circulates in the soil. In tight clay soils, six inches is sometimes as deep as feeder roots can go, though twelve and eighteen inches are more common. In sandy soils, roots typically grow deep until they hit a clay layer. The standard talk of forty-foot-deep roots is "bunkum," according to some experts I've consulted. Such rumors got started, they say, by scientists walking through cuts and stream banks, seeing roots at the bottom of the cuts. Along a forty-foot bank, you might see tree roots all the way to the bottom; that's because aeration is good along the sides of the bank.

Everyone knows that underwatering is bad because it causes roots to dry out. Overwatering is equally damaging because it drives air out of the soil. The best way to water a tree is to let a hose drip on the base slowly. Overnight is great. Let the top inch of soil dry out, and then repeat the slow soaking. Do this for the first two summers after your tree has been transplanted.

Forget These Old Ideas

For years, the common wisdom in transplanting included a lot of practices we now know to be either useless or harmful.

Do not stake, except in dire circumstances where there are excessive winds and loose soil. *Do not* prune out one-third of the tree—the more leaves you have making food (photosynthesizing) for regrowing roots, the better. *Do not* wrap the trunk; it traps moisture and invites insect damage. And, finally, *do not* plant periwinkles or impatiens around the base of the tree; you'll tend to overwater the tree. A top-dressing of mulch around the trunk is perfect.

The Biggest No-No

Do not use a weed-whacker near the trunk, as it can damage the bark and girdle the tree. This common mistake accounts for more tree deaths than anything else.

〜

Help Stamp Out Plant Abuse!

〜

Sally and Andy

We have the ASPCA (American Society for the Prevention of Cruelty to Animals); it's high time we had an ASPCP for plants! Give us a dollar for every tree or shrub that has been pruned to look like a French poodle, mushroom, lollypop, or Sumerian ziggurat and we could finance George Lucas's next two film projects.

Okay, we'll admit that this is all very subjective. There are perfectly nice people who give to charities, call their mothers every Sunday, and wouldn't consider using naughty words—who really like topiary (that's what they call it when shrubs and trees are pruned into rabbits and elephants and all sorts of geometric shapes). They even pay good money for someone to come out regularly to inflict this questionable art on their innocent plants.

Art is how many people view topiary. In 1712, Dezallier D'Argenville wrote in his *Theory and Practice of Gardening*, "This topiary is the richest and most distinguished in the whole business of gardening." And author Barbara Gallup calls it "enchanting." On the other hand, nineteenth-century

"It used to be a tree."

architect William Robinson referred to it as "graceless and inert." We have a friend—a landscape architect—who detests topiary; he calls it "plant abuse," and thinks people who practice it should be sentenced to a year with a bad barber.

No matter how you feel about topiary, you can thank Cnaius Matius for creating it. He was a close buddy of Julius Caesar, which meant that he was very influential. Soon everyone was doing topiary and it became *de rigueur* at every fashionable Roman estate.

During the Dark Ages, topiary went into decline, along with just about everything else in Europe. But then, during the Italian Renaissance, topiary had a rebirth of popularity—apparently because folks lacked a wide range of plant materials. If they wanted variety in their gardens, they achieved it with clippers and fertile imaginations.

Topiary came to America around 1690 with geometric forms displayed in many Williamsburg gardens. Today, some of the most extravagant examples can be found at Longwood Gardens in Pennsylvania and Callaway Gardens in Georgia.

Why do we practice topiary? Perhaps the best answer comes from garden writer Miles Hadfield, who said that topiary is a style of gardening "which violently defies nature to show man's domination of it." Very likely. But what we know for sure about topiary is that, one: it's a lot of work, whether you do it yourself or pay to have it done. And, two: it is definitely not what Mother Nature had in mind.

Lots of people who have "lollypops" and "mushrooms" in their yards never intended to. "Oh, it's just something the landscape maintenance people did," they say. Or, "We bought the house like this." They think that once a tree or shrub has been clipped in that fashion, they have to live with it forever.

Personally, we think that these abused shrubs and small trees are attractive enough to stand on their own merits. Take the yaupon holly (*Ilex vomitoria*). Despite its Latin name, it can be a real stunner—especially the females, which display red berries all winter. The yaupon has the potential to grow twenty-five feet tall and thirty feet wide, but this process can take more than fifty years. Because it's a slow grower, most designers plan on its occupying an area about fifteen feet by fifteen feet. At that size, it fits nicely against the front of the house. It perfectly rounds off the front corners, even when you have a one-story home. It also fits nicely into those small, dark side gardens that must look good all year because they are seen from the master bedroom or the dining room.

But, in all of these instances, it is the natural spreading grace of the yaupon, or whatever tortured evergreen you possess, that makes it visually appealing. A landscape is supposed to have flow and harmony. A "lollypop" stops the flow; it is a staccato note that disrupts the rhythm.

If you've got topiary in your yard, and you think we're full of beans, that's okay. Just turn to the next chapter while we tell the rest of the readers about Sally's simple yet effective plan for pruning trees correctly and getting them back on the right track.

Sally's Sure-Fire Lollypop Restoration Plan

1. You'll need two pruners: a long-handled pair about two feet long, and a smaller one-handed pair, about nine inches long.
2. Now, check the trunks. If two are growing into each other and rubbing off bark (providing an opening for infection), keep the trunk that is growing outward, removing the trunk that is growing inward. Cut it back to ground level. Check the aesthetic quality of the trunks that are left. Be very cautious about taking out trunks that are not potential problems. Have someone pull the trunk in question as far out of the way as possible, so you can see what the tree would look like without it. If you are still in doubt, leave it. You can always remove it later, but you can't glue it back on.
3. Now, start cutting off all of the branches that grow in toward the center of the tree. Cut every one of them off at the collar—that's the slight thickening of the branch where it joins a larger branch or trunk. The idea here is to give the tree a nice, airy, open feel in the middle.
4. If the branches have been cut back so many times that the branching looks like a starburst of minibranches (a very ugly look), cut back to the first long, undamaged branch that points outward.
5. Do not cut off the end of a branch for at least five years; this allows the branches to grow long enough to give your evergreen tree structure. After five years, if your tree is as large as you want, you can begin cutting off end branches—but always cut them off at a collar. Do not just snip off an end.

In the southern half of the country, most trees and shrubs can be safely pruned at any time of year, although be cautious of pruning in November;

you don't want to stimulate tender new growth just before the first vicious winter storm. If you live in the northern half of the country, you probably don't want to prune after Labor Day.

And, never paint the cuts. They gray over very quickly, and infection is usually not a problem. If it is, use clear furniture varnish or lacquer instead of the nasty black stuff.

You'll be amazed and pleased at how much better your topiary-ed tree or shrub will look instantly. And after about a month of new growth, it will look even better. Your tree or shrub is probably drawing a sigh of relief just knowing you're reading this and getting ready to end its embarrassment.

Leave Those Leaves

❧

Sally

I'm going to let you in on a fabulous product for your lawn and garden. It covers your yard all winter and slowly decomposes, so that by spring you'll have a marvelous, all-natural-composted mulch. But that's not all. This product not only feeds and renews your soil, it also helps the spring rains soak into the soil better and then helps retain moisture in the soil during the hot summer months. It hasn't been advertised anywhere, and it's not for sale in any nursery or hardware store.

"What is this miracle product?" you're probably asking as you reach for your wallet. "Where can I buy it?"

Well, you can't buy it. It's free, and every fall you'll find mountains of it lying all over your yard. That's right, I'm talking about leaves. The same ones you rake up and stuff into those sturdy, nonbiodegradable plastic bags, and then have hauled off to the city landfill where, generations from now, archeologists will view the results of your weekend's toil.

We've got to stop thinking of those fallen leaves as trash. Leaves are Mother Nature's way of protecting the roots of plants from winter freezes. Fallen leaves are also nature's fertilizer.

If you have deciduous trees on or very near your property, let their leaves lie where they fall until after the first frost, when your perennial garden turns into a tangle of brown stalks. Then, cut down the stalks to about four inches and rake those leaves in lightly and gently. Don't pack them down; you want lots of air to get trapped in between the leaves. This air remains warmer than the outside temperature, not unlike the way air trapped under a down comforter keeps us cozy. Loose leaves also allow enough light and air to reach the soil so that perennials that maintain rosettes of green leaves all winter are happy, too.

If you have five feet or so of leaves, or even one foot, but they're not quickly breaking down in early spring, sprinkle compost starter over them. If you suspect your soil is already dead (see chapter 11), sprinkle compost starter on the soil in the fall.

The leaves you don't rake into your beds can just stay on your lawn all winter where they'll slowly decompose and turn into duff—that's how new soil begins. Of course, your unenlightened neighbors may have a fit. (Although, have you noticed? There really does seem to be less of a clean-lawn fetish abroad in the land these days.) So, if you'd prefer to take a less confrontational approach (after all, you may need to borrow a cup of sugar someday), simply rake up those leaves and put them into a compost pile in your backyard.

After they've composted, spread them back on the lawn or use them in flowerbeds or vegetable gardens. You'll find that this works just as well as using store-bought products and it's environmentally much more attractive.

Back in those dim dark days of yesteryear when Andy and I still had a lawn, we at least never used chemical fertilizers. We had a neighbor, though, who hired one of those lawn care companies to come out regular as clockwork to treat her yard with big helpings of the stuff. Frankly, we never thought that her lawn looked any better than ours. But we did notice that three fine shade trees on her property died prematurely within two years of her starting the service.

We had plenty of large deciduous trees, so there was never a leaf shortage around our house. You may not be so lucky. In that case, our advice is to steal some. Well, not actually steal, but go out and cruise your neighborhood. When you see plastic sacks of leaves set on the curb or in the alley, do a good deed. Put them on your own lawn and save space in your city's landfill.

PART IV

A Native for Every Niche

All things have their place,
knew we how to place them.

GEORGE HERBERT

Nature's laws affirm instead of prohibit. If you
violate her laws, you are your own prosecutor,
attorney, judge, jury, and hangman.

—LUTHER BURBANK

"Well, you may plant wild flowers if you like,
but personally I prefer the tame ones."

21

~

. . . And So to Bedding

~

Sally

If use translates into popularity, the most popular flowers in the plant kingdom—certainly the most ubiquitous—have to be bedding plants, such as petunias, marigolds, impatiens, periwinkles, and begonias. Everybody, it seems, uses and apparently likes these petite beauties.

Landscape architects and landscape maintenance contractors like bedding plants; it's difficult to think of an office building that doesn't have the obligatory massed array of bedding plants around the main entrance. Nursery owners like them because they are very profitable; a myriad of flats are sold every time the seasons change, usually three times a year.

Amateur gardeners like these plants because they adapt so well to the confines of a modest suburban home lot; it takes only a few to make an attractive accent by a front door or an edging by a walk or patio. Even gardening connoisseurs, who insist on variety and originality in their displays, use bedding plants to fill in bare spots and to help out abused areas near walkways.

It's easy to see why bedding plants are so popular. They're very well behaved, forming neat mounds barely over a foot across and usually a little under a foot high. Many of them bloom like crazy for months on end without a break. And they adapt well to any rich, organically well-prepared, well-drained garden soil. And then, of course, perhaps the biggest reason of all: You don't have to be a Luther Burbank to use them; they thrive for the grayest thumbs among us.

Often these flowers are annuals, but even more often they are perennials that are used as annuals where the winters are too cold for them or the summers too hot. The problem is, we use them so often that we run the risk of becoming bored with them. The most beautiful piece of music will eventually put you to sleep or drive you nuts if it's all that you hear.

So, I would like to introduce you to a few bedding plants with which you may not be familiar. Or, if you *are* familiar with them, you haven't been exposed to them enough to be jaded. Unlike most of the bedding plants you know already that come from tropical and subtropical lands, these plants are native to the southwestern United States. They're more drought-resistant than the bedding plants currently being marketed (except perhaps for portulaca and purslane). This means they'll save you water—which also means they'll save you money. Furthermore, unlike overbred impatiens and begonias, they provide important nectar for butterflies and pollen for bees.

Blackfoot daisy (*Melampodium leucanthum*) was virtually unknown when *Requiem* first came out. At that time I fearlessly predicted that it was going to become one of the most popular bedding plants in the country—once everyone found out about it. Today it's well on its way. It's a tidy plant—well behaved and always less than a foot tall and not much wider. Its small, narrow leaves are a soft green and are almost hidden by the masses of white daisylike flowers. These flowers cover the neat mounded plant from early spring, through the summer, and until late fall, usually until Thanksgiving and sometimes later, depending on when you get your first hard freeze.

Blackfoot daisy is native from Mexico to Colorado and Kansas. It's a perennial, so if it doesn't freeze to death where you live, you won't have to plant it again next year. Those from Colorado will obviously have more cold-tolerance, while those from Arizona will have the most drought-tolerance. See how logical Mother Nature is?

Blackfoot daisy is not picky about its soil, as long as it's very well drained. It will grow in poor rocky soil or sandy soil, but it is especially fond of rich garden soil that is loaded with organic matter.

Give it plenty of sun; it doesn't care for shade. This daisy will tolerate reflected heat, a very useful feature. That makes it ideal for edging a flower border next to a large paved area, such as a driveway or the deck around a swimming pool. Not only does it always look good, but it is also delightfully scented. On really hot afternoons, it smells of strong, wild honey.

Yellow plains zinnia (*Zinnia grandiflora*) is another one of my favorites. Also a perennial, it is native in the same states as blackfoot daisy, but it is not so fond of compost and prefers fast-draining soil mixes. The narrow leaves are almost threadlike, much narrower than those of the little orange-flowered Mexican *Zinnia linearis*. They are packed densely to form mats of foliage about eight inches in height that look a little like thrift (*Phlox subulata*). The flowers are about one inch in diameter, single, four-petaled, and bright yellow. The nectar is sweet and extremely popular with butterflies.

Yellow plains zinnia likes a lot of sun and blooms best when the weather is hot—May through October. It forms new plants by the roots, but it spreads too slowly to be invasive. I've heard that with patience, however, you can encourage it to become a first-class groundcover or use it like thyme between flagstones. Very similar is the dwarf white zinnia (*Zinnia acerosa*).

A taller and more open yellow daisy is **chocolate daisy** (*Berlandiera lyrata*). Native to the same states as blackfoot daisy and yellow plains zinnia, it has the extra bonus of actually smelling like chocolate. And it's not a wimpy sniff. You can bask in the aroma of baking brownies from thirty feet away.

Another fragrant flower is **mesa greggia** (*Nerisyrenia camporum*). It stands nine to twelve inches tall and is native to the Chihuahuan Desert. Its half-inch four-petaled flowers open pure white, but gradually flush pale pink and turn to rose pink before they wither. The result is a lovely combination of white and pink, often visited by white butterflies.

Golden globe (*Hymenoxys odorata*) is a showy deep yellow bouquet of flowers, sometimes given the unappreciative name bitterweed. Ranchers tend to bestow that name on several species that have foliage that tastes bitter to cattle and can make cow's milk taste like medicine to us. If you see a pasture filled with golden globe, it has not aggressively taken over the whole area and crowded out the other plants. The cows merely gobbled up the tastier plants, and only the golden globe was left to hold the soil together. So, don't be afraid to buy this very pretty flower; it will not engulf all of the other flowers in your garden.

Golden globe is an annual that is native from Kansas to California south to Mexico. It forms a one-foot ball of aromatic lime-green, finely cut foliage. The yellow daisies with large yellow centers are one to two inches in diameter and, at times, will almost completely hide the leaves. With occasional watering and snipping, it can be coaxed into blooming from early spring to a killing frost. It (like all the others in this chapter) prefers full sun and good drainage.

Desert marigold (*Baileya multiradiata*) is also a yellow daisy, but it has layers and layers of petals on long slender stems, making it an excellent cut flower. Its leaves are covered with fine silvery wool and mass closely together to form a low, fuzzy gray-green mound. The delicate stems radiate out of the mound to a height of approximately one foot. A true desert plant, this excellent flower is in bloom whenever the weather is above freezing. It usually lives from one to two years, literally blooming itself to death and dying of exhaustion. It seeds out fairly easily, and new plants are usually in bloom within three months.

Of course, this is just a sampling. Already well known is the California gold poppy. Already hybridized (with similar plants from other countries) into countless cultivars are the lavender-to-purple verbenas, and the orange-and-yellow lantana. And out there, if you're willing to look, are many, many other natives that are ready, willing, and able to go to bed in your garden.

∽

Cenizo and Friends

∽

Sally

When we wrote the first edition, this chapter had to do with introducing southwesterners to the beauties of Texas Ranger and other cenizos (*Leucophyllum* spp). It's good to see that things can change. My dear friend and mentor, the late Benny J. Simpson, horticulturist in residence at the Agricultural Division of the Texas Research Foundation in Renner, north of Dallas, Texas, developed four cenizos for the nursery market. Ron Gass, another friend of ours and the owner of Mountain States Wholesale Nursery in Glendale, Arizona, grew them in quantity and added a few Mexican cenizos.

Cenizos are now exactly where these two pioneers hoped they would be—as ubiquitous in gardens as the irrigation-dependent evergreen shrubs they have replaced. Jill Nokes, author of *How to Grow Native Plants of Texas and the Southwest*, remarked recently: "Wouldn't Benny laugh to know that we're now as tired of seeing cenizos as we were of seeing waxleaf ligustrums!"

Of course, we're really not bored with cenizos. It's painful to see them occasionally carved into cubes and spheres, but they're lovely silver-leaved evergreen shrubs with vivid flowers in royal purple, lavender, rose, or white. They're saving water, feeding bees, and they don't require pesticides.

What hasn't sufficiently changed is what homeowners plant alongside their cenizos. Many are being overwatered, because the concept of grouping plants according to their water needs is still not fully understood.

Homeowners in this country's desert regions (basically everyone from El Paso west to Los Angeles and San Diego in Zones 8–10) seem to have two basic approaches to landscaping: They either fill their yards with rocks, gravel, and cacti, or they try to copy landscapes in Virginia and Connecticut, with carpets of thirsty lawns and all sorts of back-east-style annuals and perennials.

Yet, they are literally surrounded by a wealth of gorgeous (not to mention low-maintenance and water-conserving) desert plants that would introduce exciting new colors and textures to their look-alike yards.

Amazingly, it isn't only homeowners who are unaware of this marvelous and available native palette. A year or so ago I gave a talk in El Paso to a group composed largely of nursery owners and landscape architects. As I proceeded through the program, flashing slide after slide on the screen, people in the audience kept interrupting to ask me to repeat a plant name or simply to express surprise that these plants had been practically in their backyards all along.

If you want to use cenizo in your landscape, remember that this is a desert plant. Give it plenty of sun and room. Mass it in a loose drift instead of lining it up in a tight row. Desert plants do not cram themselves together like those found in a Louisiana bottomland woods. They like plenty of light and air circulation.

And please, do not overwater it. Use companion plants that are also drought-resistant; putting cenizo next to water-guzzlers like St. Augustine or fescue is not a great idea. Asian jasmine, flowers that require weekly watering, and other plants that prefer more than thirty-five inches of rain a year do not belong near a cenizo either. Cenizos can thrive gloriously on twenty inches and sustain themselves attractively on a mere ten.

Take into consideration the aesthetics of leaf texture, foliage colors, and the shorter heights of plants associated with cenizo. Because cenizo has silvery leaves, use other plants that echo that color. Artemesia (there are various kinds), Arizona cypress, bursage (*Ambrosia* spp.), and silver dalea (*Dalea bicolor* var. *argyraea*) are some good choices that are fairly easy to find.

For contrast, use plants with dark green foliage, such as evergreen sumac (*Rhus virens*), littleleaf sumac (*Rhus microphylla*), the large-leaved sumac called sugar bush (*Rhus ovata*), Texas mountain laurel (*Sophora secundiflora*), Apache plume (*Fallugia paradoxa*), or creosote (*Larrea tridentata*). Mix in a few with yellow-green foliage like mesquite and goldenball lead tree (*Leucena retusa*) or those with lime-green trunks and branches such as paloverde and retama (*Parkinsonia* spp.).

At the base of your garden, use a mulch of local multi-sized and multi-colored rocks; avoid lava rocks, dyed pebbles, or pea gravel. The idea is to look natural. And forget the black plastic underneath; instead plant a scattering of wildflowers and short tufts of native grasses such as buffalograss, Indian ricegrass, sideoats grama, or blue grama among the rocks.

There are many flowers that look especially good with cenizo. Its own flowers are soft pink to lavender to royal purple; one selection has white blooms. White-flowered perennials such as blackfoot daisy carry on the silvery color scheme, but my favorite combination includes orange, purple, red, and hot pink flowers for accents.

There are a variety of penstemons (*Penstemon* spp.) that bloom in early spring in reds and strong pinks. Later in the season, globemallows (*Sphaeralcea* spp.) provide easy masses of bright orange-red satiny flowers that require only intermittent deep waterings to keep blooming all summer and fall. A profusion of salvias (*Salvia* spp.), including the shrubby and popular *Salvia greggii*, are also good companion plants. And don't forget all those yellow daisies such as chocolate daisy (*Berlandiera lyrata*), desert marigold (*Balieya multiridiata*), paperflower (*Psilostrophe tagetina*), and zexmenia (*Wedelia texana*).

You may be the last one on your block to plant cenizo, but once your neighbors see all the companion plants you've chosen, you can still be a trendsetter.

23

❧

Grass Roots Support
for Buffalograss

❧

Andy

A while back, we were dining with friends, an unmarried couple we'll call John and Mary. They'd been dating for years with no hint of wedding bells—a situation that was clearly more vexing to Mary than to John. At one point in the evening's conversation, the topic of matrimony came up. We both swear we didn't mention it; we're not that crazy.

Well, one thing led to another and soon John was feeling like a murdered heiress' sleazy-looking husband being grilled by Perry Mason. At one point, Mary just confronted him with the BIG question: "How come you're so afraid of commitment?" she asked.

John babbled on, offering one lame defense after another. Finally, he blurted out, "Okay, you want to know the real reason? It's my weekends! First, you get married. Then, you get a house. And that means a lawn! And that means mowing and watering and . . . and . . . that means my weekends will be ruined forever!"

I could have kept my mouth shut. But, no, I immediately and enthusiastically launched into a sales pitch for buffalograss, a turf grass that is becoming synonymous with low maintenance. Buffalograss may not make lawnmowers obsolete, but they'll definitely be spending a lot more time in the tool shed. John's bachelor days were numbered!

Buffalograss (*Buchloe dactyloides*) was not named for the city in upstate New York. It was, instead, misnamed for those hairy mammals that once roamed our prairies (of course, we all know they're really bison).

Buffalograss is native throughout the Great Plains, from Minnesota to Montana and as far south as—believe it or not—Central America—wherever conditions aren't too moist, too shady, or too sandy. Some of the newer varieties are being tested and used all over the country, from California to New Jersey.

In Poland, where I was born, there is buffalograss vodka. (This is a case of two plants having the same common name but being of two different species.) A stalk of the European buffalograss is put into the bottle, giving the vodka a distinctive flavor and a light amber hue. Back in the 1970s, the FDA outlawed the importation of this vodka because it feared that terrible little creatures would enter our country on the stalks. (As if anything could live in that potent drink!) But now it is once again available in some liquor stores.

In the right environment, maintaining a buffalograss lawn is a cinch. Make sure it gets a lot of sun, and give it just enough water in the summer to keep it green. You'll find that it needs less water than naturalized Bermuda and Kentucky bluegrass, and 50 to 80 percent less than is needed to keep St. Augustine alive and well. That's why water departments love buffalograss. It fits in perfectly with the xeriscape concept.

Buffalograss is tough, and it can take a lot of foot traffic. At the same time, however, it's quite attractive, with a very pretty, fine, soft, even texture that invites bare feet. It covers quickly, needs less fertilizer, and outlives conventional turf grasses. Plugged clones may form such a dense sod that weeds can't get a root in edgewise; pure stands in the wild are quite common. Furthermore, it stays out of your flowerbed; its roots are not at all invasive.

Buffalograss can be kept at a typical two-inch height, so as not to offend your neighbors, or it can be allowed to grow to its full eight to fifteen inches (depending on the variety) for use in a meadow or, for the more daring among you, as a beautifully undulating blue-green sea in front of your house. Most people let it grow to three or four inches and mow it just twice a year—the first time after spring's initial burst of growth when numerous stolons and runners are produced, and then again in the Fall. One homeowner we met puts the training wheels from his kid's bike on his mower to cut his buffalograss at a six-inch height.

Come frost, or when the weather gets too dry, buffalograss will go dormant and turn a soft golden brown. The male flowers, a great part of its visual appeal, are visible even through the winter.

For years, the only buffalograss you could buy had been bred for pastures and had been selected for height, "Texoka," "Comanche," and "Sharp's Improved" being the best known. It's not that cattle don't like to stoop down; taller grass simply means more cow-chow per acre. These strains are excellent for use in meadows, but at one point water-conscious homeowners thought it would be a good idea to use them for lawns.

Buffalograss is extremely heat- and cold-resistant, drought-tolerant, and requires minimal fertilization and pesticide control. The cultivars have been selected to spread rapidly and green earlier than St. Augustine and Bermuda. A bonus for hayfever sufferers: because "Prairie" and "609" are female grasses, there's no pollen.

As sometimes happens when a good idea starts taking hold, the good idea gets even better. By the early 1990s, several new varieties came on the market, designed to look even more lawnlike. "Prairie" was developed at Texas A&M by Dr. Milt Engelke, and "609" was developed by Dr. Terry Riordan at the University of Nebraska. Both grow to a maximum height of eight to ten inches and continue to sell well.

"Stampede," another new variety, grows to just four inches. These are being followed into the marketplace by other cultivars, such as "Cody" and "Bowie," both suited to the Midwest. There are now also more cold-hardy varieties for the northern state—"Legacy" being the most popular. And the University of California has recently come up with a variety called "UC Verde," which was developed especially for coastal California landscapes.

Dr. David Huff (associate professor of Plant Genetics at Pennsylvania State University) developed a unique strain of a short-leafed buffalograss from Mexico—a diploid that delivers greater density—and an all-male short turf variety that comes with different colored anthers; he already has red, white, and blue separated. Imagine *that* planted in front of the White House.

Admittedly, enthusiasm for buffalograss varies across the nation, from "the greatest thing since blue corn chips" in the Southwest, to "promising, but the jury is still out" up north. Dr. Huff gives buffalograss a qualified thumbs-up for the Northeast. He gives buffalograss high marks for toughness and low maintenance, particularly in compacted, heavy soils. He cites as an example an accidental plot that took hold at Rutgers University in New Jersey in the early 1980s. It seems that another turf professor came to Rutgers from Oklahoma but decided not to pursue his buffalograss research in the Garden State, tossing his seeds into the nearest garbage dumpster. Well, not all of the seeds made it into the trash. Today, that plot of buffalograss is doing very well with no maintenance at all. This resulted, according to Huff, in the state of New Jersey expressing interest in using buffalograss along the Turnpike and the Garden State Parkway, on steep unmowable slopes.

Connie and Glenn Suhren, in Garland, Texas, qualify as true believers. They broadcast "Texoka" seed by hand in April 1987, when their new house was surrounded by bare earth. Four months later, they had an attractive, verdant lawn. It probably would have spread more quickly in better soil, but the Suhrens had a lot of caliche in their yard.

To get it established, the Suhrens watered only twice a week (it was a particularly wet spring), and then cut back to just twice a month or whenever the soil felt dry. Normally, once established, buffalograss stays green on a couple of waterings a summer. Many of the Suhrens's neighbors, according to Connie, water their conventional lawns every other day.

In fact, the biggest problem buffalograss advocates face is convincing new users not to treat it in the same way as conventional turf grasses. They tend to overwater it, making it weedy. When they see that, they conclude that it isn't any good.

As for mowing (another big advantage for those of us who can easily think of several hundred other things we'd rather be doing), Glenn Suhrens cuts his lawn every three or four weeks, putting the mower on the highest setting. He claims the neighbors are out there every week cutting their Bermuda—sometimes more often.

For many people around the country, especially those who live in the West and the Midwest, buffalograss will provide that low-maintenance lawn they've always wanted. But is it the answer to every homeowner's dream? Obviously not. If your property is full of big shade trees, buffalograss won't make it; it needs lots of sun.

In the final analysis, the right lawn for you has to be determined by weighing all of the pros and cons of each turf grass in your region. When you select your turf grass, drought-tolerance should be considered, as well as cold-tolerance, soil types and conditions . . . and, of course, plain ole' visual appeal.

As for John and Mary . . . well, they eventually did get married. They bought a condo.

⁓

Mexican Hat:
A Black-Thumb Perennial

⁓

Sally

You probably think that anyone who writes a gardening book has to be a terrific gardener. I can't speak for other authors, but I'm of the black-thumb variety and Andy doesn't even try!

My paternal grandmother was a *gardener*. She had the gift. The touch. Granny would stick something into the ground, give it a little water, and that was it. She never seemed to work very hard at her gardening, yet year after year all kinds of flowers and shrubs would flourish under her care. Even during droughts. Nothing ever died by accident in Granny's garden.

I definitely didn't get the right genes. My gardens are quite different; death is not uncommon there. The way I see it, if a plant can survive in spite of my care, *anyone* can grow it successfully.

Mexican hat (*Ratibida columnifera*) is just such a plant. It grows anywhere from Minnesota to, as you'd expect, Mexico. So right off you know it's tolerant of a wide range of conditions. It starts blooming when it gets warm in the spring and keeps on blooming until frost, and often blossoms even *after* frost, until it gets knocked back by a hard freeze.

Mexican hat makes a good cut flower; it can last a week, and the long slender stems make it easy to arrange. Each flower is shaped like a sombrero, hence its name. The "brim" has petals that are usually maroon around the base and yellow at the tips. Occasionally, the maroon part is orange or chocolate, and sometimes the petals are all yellow or all maroon. The tall, narrow cone, or "crown," of Mexican hat consists of the tiny yellow flowers that get fertilized to make seed. In the fall, the old cones that bloomed in late spring or early summer have turned gray, and you can easily crumble them to release dozens of ripe seeds.

These germinate easily, and one plant can provide enough to fill an acre. To sow the seed, scratch the soil lightly, scatter the seeds, and cover them with soil to the thickness of the seed (about one millimeter), and then give the soil a gentle pat. If planted in the fall, the flowers will appear the first summer.

The whole plant is normally vase-shaped, but this varies according to its environment. On rocky limestone slopes or in hot, unwatered sandy soils, it is about twelve to fourteen inches tall and well-shaped. It stays fresher and blooms longer if it is given afternoon shade but will probably not bloom in August and early September until the weather cools off or there is some rain.

In rich, irrigated garden soil, Mexican hat makes a luxuriant ferny mound two feet tall and two feet wide. In these conditions, it will bloom steadily throughout the hottest part of the summer. If it gets too much shade and moisture, it may develop mildew, become leggy, and flop over. (Even easy plants have limits.) If the plant has endured drought, the top leaves will wither and new leaves will form at the base. This is how Mexican hat prefers to survive the winter.

However, without drought, the rich ferny mound is capable of staying green through a mild winter. If it dies in a harsh one, don't worry. Dozens of small plants should be on their way from seed that gets shattered and scattered in the fall. If you are a basic pessimist, sow a little seed yourself each year after it has ripened.

If Mexican hat doesn't work for you—well, we understand they're doing wonderful things these days with plastic.

∽

Putting Ferns in
Their Proper Place

∽

Sally

Think of ferns and you probably think of indoor hanging baskets—restaurant decor or window dressing for your breakfast nook. Keep in mind that these ferns are imports from humid climes, often tropical. I've been in plenty of restaurants and homes that are warm enough for tropical ferns, but none that are humid enough to qualify as suitable fern habitat. So, now you know why your ferns need a lot of grooming and watering and spritzing—a degree of dedication I lack, which means my own ferns die at an alarming rate.

Besides, as the cliched observation goes: "Mother Nature didn't make any indoor plants." And that includes ferns. Ferns evolved outdoors, and they can provide marvelous accents and textures in your garden.

They can even serve as an attractive groundcover if you live in a part of the country where the ground stays moist all year. Moisture is the key to success with ferns. In Canada—which is seldom confused with the tropics—you can find vast and lush fern carpets on the forest floors. What makes them lush is that they get plenty of moisture. And, because they're native to that area, they can handle the Canadian winters.

The ferns that will grow best for you are the ones that are native to your area—the very ones that are being ignored by the nursery trade and home gardeners alike.

You can find ferns growing naturally all over our country, in upland woods, in bogs, and alongside springs and waterways. The ones most usable for landscapes (those more than one foot tall) are native to areas that have an annual rainfall of more than thirty-five inches. Of course, you'll find equally large ferns in areas with less rainfall, but in those cases the temperatures tend to be lower to compensate.

Believe it or not, you can find ferns in the desert, although they aren't really growing in the desert habitat itself; they are clinging to canyon walls where they find dependable seeps, shaded by cliffs or woodland. Those ferns that grow where the seeps are shallow and dependent on rainfall grow small, about the size of your hand. And, even though these ferns are a delight to discover on a nature hike, they aren't really suitable for most gardens.

Some ferns are more drought-tolerant than others, but they are all vulnerable to drought to some degree, and that's because they're so shallow-rooted. When a drought occurs and ferns get too dry, they are programmed to go dormant and wait for better and wetter days. If dry conditions persist, a few ferns in the colony will actually die; the whole colony can die if the drought goes on a long time.

Most ferns grow in colonies because they reproduce easily by the roots. They can even be somewhat aggressive when conditions are properly moist and cool. A healthy colony of ferns can advance approximately one foot each year—this is important to know when you are buying only a few ferns and you want them to fill a larger space.

Ferns are notoriously hard to transplant, but talented gardeners can get them started in the greenhouse from root cuttings. When ferns are grown from spores, the process is much slower. Each fern releases millions of microscopic spores each year in late summer. On a dry, breezy day, the spores float out into the world, hoping to find a moist shady spot.

The tiny fraction that are successful are still a long way from becoming ferns. First, they have to grow gametophytes, quarter-inch, heart-shaped plants that also have to grow, producing a fertile egg. Only a few of these eggs live long enough to develop successfully into adults. How's that for a precarious and convoluted method of reproduction!

Nurseries that stock outdoor ferns usually have a pretty scanty selection—one or two kinds—and, all too often, most of those choices are from Japan.

That's a shame. We have so many lovely native ferns, with a wide range of heights, textures, and habits and a range of colors from golden green to dramatic dark green. Some are very polite, while others will seize an acre and make it their own.

In order to describe some of the most hardy and widespread of these ferns to you, I will divide them into two groups. First there are those that can grow in shallow water and tight clay soils and can tolerate poor drainage. And then there are those that require plenty of moisture but good drainage and lots of oxygen at the same time, growing only in sandy loam or on rocky slopes.

Poor drainage ferns are the easiest to grow. You need only worry about whether they are getting enough water, not that they are receiving too *much*. These ferns may be planted around the edge of a pond, under a birdbath, and in those areas around the foundation of your house where moss appears on its own. In a typically level garden, you can dig out a shallow hollow to plant them in. Then, watering is a snap; just let the hose run until the hollow is filled. Repeat only when the soil becomes almost dry. A top dressing of compost is a good idea; it feeds the roots and helps hold in moisture.

The two osmunda ferns are the largest and most distinctive. Cinnamon fern (*Osmunda cinnamomea*) is two to five feet tall and will grow as wide. It is native from Newfoundland to Texas to South America. The roots gradually make huge mounds of osmunda fiber that stick up out of the bog. These ferns can grow to be very old. In fact, one source I read implied that they might be "immortal." The leaves are twice cut, which means the overall effect is fine textured. The fertile fronds are cinnamon in color.

Royal fern (*Osmunda regalis* var. *spectabilis*) gets three to six feet tall. It is native from eastern North America to South America. It is most often found just out of the bog, on the squishy banks above the cinnamon ferns. It grows very well in a garden setting and, because of its height, it makes a dramatic backdrop for smaller ferns. Place one or more together to form a clump in a corner where you need more height. The leaves are of a coarser texture, only once divided, and the fertile fronds are golden.

Lady fern (*Athyrium filix-femina*) grows two to six feet high. It can be fairly aggressive and makes a good groundcover. Its height makes it useful around a deck, or as a prominent mass at the end of the garden. The leaves are finely divided to give the fronds a lacy appearance. It has varieties native to both western and eastern North America.

Chain fern (*Woodwardia areolata*) is one of my favorites. It's usually only about a foot tall, although it can reach two and one-half feet in very rich soil. It has a very simple leaf and makes a soothing groundcover, perfect for setting off the taller, more richly textured ferns. I often see this fern growing on the soggy slopes around the royal fern. It is most prevalent from Massachusetts to east Texas.

These ferns, each with its own height and texture, are especially pretty when combined with one another.

In the Pacific Northwest, the other fern-growing center for North America, the easiest fern to grow in bogs, even sphagnum bogs, is deer fern (*Blechnum spicant*). It will also grow in moist woods. Similar to sword fern (described below), deer fern has narrower dark green fronds that taper at tip and base. In summer, the fertile fronds make a distinctive bouquet in the center.

Good drainage ferns need shade. They do best in rocky or sandy soils, in raised beds, or on slopes, as they cannot tolerate standing water or soggy soils. If they grow in water, that water must be constantly moving and freshly laden with air. These ferns are considerably more drought-tolerant than the bog ferns, but that's a relative statement; they can never be allowed to dry out completely without the risk of loss. Don't plan to use these as a groundcover in unwatered situations, unless you live in the mountains or so far north that summer temperatures rarely get over 90°F.

Sensitive fern (*Onoclea sensibilis*)—a name that acknowledges its tendency to curl its fronds when touched—is also called bead fern, the "beads" referring to spikes laden with beadlike spore sacs that remain after the leaves have frozen to the ground in winter. Sensitive fern prefers loose, sandy soils and is always seen on the sloping sides of wet places. It is one foot tall in regular garden soil and might reach three feet in heavily composted beds. It has a very coarse texture, so it is usually best used farther from the house. It can be fairly aggressive, which means it makes an easy groundcover for large spaces. It is native from eastern Canada west to Manitoba and south to the Gulf of Mexico.

There are two predominant maidenhair ferns in the United States. Both grow in moist, loose-soiled, well-drained beds or on moist slopes. Both have wiry black stems and small, distinctive fan-shaped leaflets. The big visual difference is the stem: the northern one forms a gentle swirl and the southern one arches but does not swirl. Both are native from coast to coast. Southern maidenhair fern (*Adiantum capillus-veneris*) is native from the Atlantic to the Pacific, from North Carolina (where it is rare) to California. Northern maidenhair fern (*Adiantum pedatum*) tends to grow down both coasts, but is better adapted to the north and skips the middle of the continent. Some botanists are now calling the western one *Adiantum aleuticum*. In the Southwest, maidenhair fern is seen only on limestone ledges or cave walls that have a continuous flow of water. It seeds out (or spores out) beautifully down moist limestone retaining walls and loves the humidity created by a waterfall.

Polystichums are mostly evergreen ferns. Christmas fern (*Polystichum acrostichoides*) is native from Nova Scotia to Mexico. Its fronds are a darker green and a simpler design than most ferns. They bunch together to make dense clumps one to two feet tall and just as broad. Consistent moisture and super drainage are musts, but if you need an evergreen fern of short stature around the house, then it's worth the extra trouble.

In the Pacific Northwest, common sword fern (*Polystichum munitum*) is easy to grow. It makes magnificent three- to five-foot-tall clumps in lowland conifer forests under Douglas fir, redwoods, and western arborvitae. Not only is it larger and more lush than Christmas fern, its dark green leaflets are so densely arranged that it has a fringed look.

Another easy fern for the Pacific Northwest is rooting chain fern (*Woodwardia fimbriata*). Very dramatic, its wide, twice-divided fronds can get six feet long. Although found in moister woods and seeps than common sword fern, it can adapt to gardens if given only a little supplemental water.

Bracken (*Pteridium aquilinum* var. *pseudocaudatum*) is the oddball of the fern family. One species populates most of the world. Since the last Ice Age, only the center of our continent has lost its bracken. Unlike the other ferns, its roots grow deep. It is most often found in poor soils and in hotter, drier conditions than other ferns can tolerate. It prefers well-drained, poor, sandy, acidic soils, although it can grow in a wide range of conditions. It is commonly two to three feet tall and forms large colonies under post oaks and pines. It can look good in dry woods with no supplemental water.

The best-known fern in the South, and the only one easily bought at many nurseries, is the wood fern (*Thelypteris kunthii*). It can thrive with only one watering a week, given sufficient shade and temperatures below 100°F. It can grow in any soil, acid or limey. However, wood fern is also one of the least winter-hardy ferns. It definitely suffers in areas where temperatures fall below 0°F.

I'm not advocating tossing all your fern baskets away. If you've got the dedication and desire to keep them alive indoors, more power to you. But, if you live in a fern-friendly environment, I hope I've inspired you to try some of the locals.

26

Saguaro:
The Ubiquitous Endemic

Andy

en·dem·ic (en-dem-ik) *adj.* Peculiar to a particular locality; indigenous.
u·biq·ui·tous (yoo-bik-wi-tes) *adj.* Present everywhere; being everywhere.

One of the last places we expected to see a saguaro cactus was up in Canada. But there it was, on a busy street in downtown Winnipeg. Okay, admittedly, it was part of a neon sign advertising a place called the Santa Fe Cafe. But that in itself was remarkable in that this cactus isn't found within 400 miles of Santa Fe!

I wasn't so much surprised as amused; for some time I'd been observing the incredible range of this towering cactus—not in any botanical sense, but as a universally accepted symbol of the West. When little kids in New Jersey, Ohio, Alabama, and Saskatchewan draw pictures of cowboys galloping across prairies and ranchlands, they invariably include a saguaro or two as part of the scenery. They almost

109

certainly don't know its name, but the image of the tall cactus with the upraised arms is very familiar.

But it's not just kids who credit this cactus with a far greater range than it actually has; it appears that almost everyone shares the misconception that the majestic, multiarmed saguaro (se-GWA-ro) is found throughout our western states. Cartoonists frequently include saguaros when drawing western scenes. Charles Schulz put one in his "Peanuts" strip whenever he showed Snoopy's brother Spike, who lives somewhere out West. And Gary Larsen often included saguaros in his cartoons depicting cowboys.

Granted, cartoonists tend to live in a fantasy world, but wouldn't you expect a large and successful corporation to be better grounded? Then explain a recent Southwest Airlines ad. The company, based in Texas since 1971, ran the ad to promote its low ticket prices. The headline announced that "*Before 1971 Low Fares Were Just Another Tall Texas Tale.*" The ad shows a cowpoke astride a jackelope—a mythical critter that is half-jackrabbit, half-antelope—and the copy explains that while the jackelope is "hard to find" in Texas, low airfares aren't. Cute—but there's not a word in the copy about the two saguaro cacti standing in the background, which are equally "hard to find" in the Lone Star State.

In fact, the saguaro (*Carnegiea gigantea*) is found in a relatively small part of the western United States. Although it appears on Arizona license plates, and its spring blooms have been designated the state's official flower, the saguaro is indigenous only in the southwestern quadrant of the state. It is the signature plant of the Sonoran Desert, which surrounds Tucson and Phoenix, and reaches into a miniscule portion of southeastern California along the Colorado River, and on down into northwestern Mexico. Even within those limited confines, the saguaro grows only at elevations between 1,500 and 3,500 feet. That's it. Try as you may, you won't find it growing naturally in any other place in the West.

But even those who grant that the saguaro is a desert plant—one of its nicknames is the "Monarch of the Desert"—frequently get it all wrong when it comes to exactly *which* desert they mean. Some misguided landscapers plant them around Las Vegas, Nevada, which is in the Mojave Desert, and where the winters are simply too cold for saguaros. Some people believe that they grow in southern New Mexico in the Chihuahuan Desert, where it is also too cold. Tourists visiting northern New Mexico, up in the Sangre De Cristo Mountains, can buy T-shirts as far north as Taos (elevation 7,400 feet) that display saguaros as if they were native to the area. And in Hamilton, Montana, you can see a seven-foot-tall saguaro (carved out of pine) in front of a local eatery.

And recently, while watching the "Today" show, I spotted one of those hand-painted hey-look-at-me signs held up above the screaming crowd of tourists. This particular sign announced that the visitor was from Oklahoma, and it was adorned with . . . you guessed it, a saguaro!

Blame the Movies

How did this notion that saguaros grow all over the West originate? The misunderstanding probably began in Hollywood. From the first silent horse operas starring the likes of Bronco Billy Anderson and Tom Mix, to all those TV oaters that dominated our TV screens back in the 1960s and 1970s, to more recent westerns, filmmakers have demonstrated a very sketchy idea of what the real West looks like. In those old westerns, actors regularly portrayed Texas Rangers, Kansas cattlemen, and California miners with saguaros as part of the backdrop. And when scenes were shot on sound stages or on studio back lots in Burbank and Culver City, the prop men created saguaros out of plaster-of-paris or carved them out of balsa wood. Directors knew that a scene just wouldn't look "authentic" without a few saguaros in view.

Just a few examples: 1950s classic *Winchester '73* starring Jimmy Stewart ends up outside a town called Tascosa, where Stewart (the good guy) and Stephen McNally (the bad guy) shoot it out amongst the saguaros and boulders of a typical Sonoran scene. Even the buildings in the town are adobe. Just one little problem; Tascosa isn't in southern Arizona, it's way up in the Texas panhandle, approximately 35 miles northwest of Amarillo!

In the 1962 epic *How the West Was Won*, there's a spectacular scene where stuntman Loren Janes gets shot off the top of a speeding train—and flies smack into a giant saguaro. But, according to the story line, the action takes place somewhere between Monument Valley, Utah, and Kingman, Arizona, some 150 miles to the north of the Sonoran Desert.

And in the 1989 Val Kilmer film, *Billy the Kid*, we are treated to a stunning opening shot of silhouetted saguaros against a burnt orange sunset. But, as any Western history buff can tell you, in real life as well as in the screenplay, Billy the Kid operated in Lincoln County, New Mexico, far to the east of the Sonoran Desert.

Chris Ousley, Film and Commercials Manager for Old Tucson movie studio, has a simple explanation. Since the facility—called the "Hollywood of the Desert"—opened for business in 1939, more than 350 cowboy movies and television shows have been filmed there, including *Rio Bravo*, *El Dorado*, *The Gunfight at the OK Corral*, and the TV series, *High Chaparral*.

"We're located in the heart of the Sonoran Desert, next door to the Saguaro National Park," says Ousley. "Frankly, it would be difficult to shoot an outdoor scene here without picking up saguaros." Besides, he adds, his clients are producers and directors, not botanists.

Old Tucson also functions as a theme park, with actors shooting it out at high noon for tourists from all over the world. "Often," says Ousley, "this is the only view of the western United States these tourists get. Naturally, our dramatic, towering saguaros make a vivid and long-lasting impression on them."

By the way, saguaros are not only misplaced in cowboy flicks; an *X-Files* episode showed saguaros in what was supposed to be New Mexico. Come to think of it, maybe it wasn't the producers who messed up—it was probably the work of ETs.

Motel Logos

Another interesting sidelight on saguaros is their widespread appeal as logos for motels. Throughout the West, mom-and-pop motels display saguaros on their signs, and often even name their inns for this cactus—even though they are located nowhere near the Sonoran Desert. There's one on Highway 40 in Denver—some 2,000 feet too high and 750 miles too far north for saguaro. And in Salt Lake City, you'll find The Covered Wagon Motel, on Highway 89. The sign features a scene depicting the 1847 Mormon migration from Illinois to Utah, and it's fairly accurate except for one small detail: there are saguaro cacti alongside the trail these pioneers are seen taking—a trail well over 600 miles out of the saguaro's native range.

Aside from being botanically inaccurate, these saguaro signs often display a remarkably sadistic streak when they also show a traditionally garbed Mexican—sombrero and serape—sleeping *against* the cactus. Picturesque, sure, but highly unrealistic due to the saguaro's sharp spines.

Other Commercial Uses

Coors Brewing Company uses the saguaro in storefront neon signs advertising their product, even though the cactus exists nowhere near their Golden, Colorado, headquarters. Old El Paso brand foods makes a line of salsas, enchilada sauces, and bean dips, and displays several saguaros as part of their logo. El Paso is, of course, in the southwestern corner of Texas, a whole state away from where saguaros grow. But then, the company is headquartered in Minneapolis, Minnesota, so what do they know!

Three saguaros even found their way into the package design for sesame-garlic Mochi (*Moh*-Chee), a traditional Japanese pocket-pastry made from short-grain sweet brown rice. The company that makes and markets this product is not, as you might guess, located in Phoenix or Tucson, but in the Bay area of California. "So how come the saguaros?" I asked Tony Plotkin, president of Grainaissance, Inc. "We wanted to de-emphasize the Japanese connection and Americanize the product," he explained. "And because the saguaro is so closely associated with the American west, we felt it was an ideal image for our purposes."

And then there's Metric Motors, an auto parts and repair shop in the mountains of Taos, New Mexico. Its sign sports a saguaro, although owner Joe Franzetti acknowledges the cactus grows nowhere near his place of business. "My ex-wife, Pozzi, designed it twenty years ago," he says. "I have no idea what she had in mind."

But as I looked at Joe's sign, it came to me. Metric specializes in foreign cars, and nothing is more foreign to Taos than the saguaro. Subtle, that Pozzi!

~

27

Sumacs for Red Fall Color

~

Sally

You Yankees have so much dazzling fall color up there (as my Yankee husband keeps reminding me), you don't give your sumacs their full due. But in the South and Southwest, it rarely gets cold enough to produce startling foliage. Also, what color there is gets rationed out in small doses over a two-month period instead of being squeezed into one or two breathtaking weeks. The satisfaction quotient just isn't the same. So, for a guaranteed bit of red autumn glory, we Southerners plant sumacs.

But you don't have to be hard up for fall color to enjoy sumacs. Everyone in North America south of the boreal forest can enjoy the exuberant glory of a sumac. We have a few evergreen sumacs that tolerate shade, but the fall-color sumacs should be planted in a sunny spot. Any soil type will do—sand, loam, caliche, clay, or limestone—as long as there is good drainage. These sumacs hate standing water or a swamp.

Flameleaf sumac (*Rhus copallinum*) is native from Maine to east Texas. Most Texans prefer to use the central Texas version: prairie flameleaf sumac (*Rhus lanceolata*). Closely related, these lovely small (ten to twenty feet) trees or tall shrubs have slender pale gray trunks, smooth and covered with white dots. Flowers in late summer display creamy white pyramids of blooms that are usually covered with butterflies. The fruits are clusters of tiny hard red berries that have a lemony flavor and are eaten by a number of birds.

There are two other sumacs similar in appearance to the flameleaf sumacs. Smooth sumac (*Rhus glabra*) makes a thicket three to ten feet tall. It can be a pest if you don't put it in the right place, as its roots are *always* on the move. I had one crawl twenty feet under a deck and then come up in a flower garden, where it was most unwelcome.

Smooth sumac is native throughout the United States, except in the deserts, and its favorite spot is on the sunny edge of a woodland. As the woods grow out and the shade extends, it travels as a thicket to maintain its position in the sun. Although not a candidate for a small garden, smooth sumac is ideal for holding an eroding slope or for creating a bird habitat in the corner of a large backyard. It grows very quickly. I've known it to start suckering only one month after being planted.

Staghorn sumac (*Rhus typhina*) grows taller—up to thirty feet—and it is more commonly found in the Northeast or in the mountains of the southeastern United States. Its branches are velvety like a stag's horns, and the leaves are large and dramatic. For the faint of heart, there is a nursery selection with a lacy leaf.

These four sumacs are very similar. And, since you'd be buying them when they are small (in one- to five-gallon containers), you'll want to know which is which. Look carefully at the leaves. They consist of a stem with numerous pairs of leaflets. The two flameleaf sumacs have a row of tiny (one-eighth- to one-fourth-inch) leafy material running along both sides of the stem. Staghorn and smooth sumac don't have these leafy margins on the stem. You can tell them apart by hairiness. Staghorn has fuzzy stems and the young leaves are fuzzy underneath. Smooth sumac is never fuzzy anywhere; it gets its name from its smooth, shiny leaves.

Our shortest sumac is the shrubby aromatic sumac or skunkbush. (Its names come from the rather spicy fragrance you get from crushing the leaves; some people like the scent and, obviously, some don't.) It's called *Rhus trilobata* in the western half of North America and *Rhus aromatica* in the eastern half. The group, as a whole, is native from the Atlantic to the Pacific and from Canada to Mexico. It doesn't look like the sumacs described above at all because its leaflets are arranged in threes. The whole leaf ranges from one to three inches broad and is sometimes fuzzy and sometimes glossy and smooth. It normally forms a well-rounded shrub about three feet tall, although I've seen old ones reach eight feet, and twelve feet has been recorded. The variety most commonly found in the nursery trade is *Rhus aromatica* var. *arenaria*. Native to the sandy shores of Lake Michigan, it is usually under three feet tall and has especially large leaves. I don't know how it fares in most of the country, but it does not seem to survive in Southwestern gardens. (See chapter 5, "An Eskimo in Death Valley.")

The aromatic sumac native to your area can be used in your garden as a single plant, but I love several of them clustered in a corner to create a bird thicket. The beauty of it is that these three-leafed sumacs make a controllable thicket because they rarely sucker except in deep loose sand.

In full sun, aromatic sumac becomes a brilliant red. Actually, it is a mosaic of reds ranging from dark red to orange red, sometimes sprinkled with green and gold. In half a day of shade, yellow and orange with touches of red is more common.

Aromatic sumac blossoms quite early in the spring with little yellow flowers; the berries ripen red in early summer and are prime bird food.

If you can't find one of these sumacs at a nursery and you plan to dig one from the wild, don't even touch it until you are sure you have identified the sumac correctly. I don't mean to sound overly dramatic, but these sumacs have poisonous relatives. Aromatic sumac has a leaf composed of three leaflets very similar to poison ivy and poison oak. The difference is that aromatic sumac has lobes only at the ends of its leaflets instead of all the way around. The smooth sumac's leaf is similar to that of poison sumac. Poison sumac has fewer leaflets, but when you are looking at eleven to thirteen leaflets, it may be either one. If you see the leafy stem of the flameleaf sumacs, you are quite safe. None of the sumacs I have recommended here will give you any kind of dermatitis.

~

Meet the Family

~

Sally

If you try to memorize the name of each plant in your area, it can be pretty intimidating; there are, after all, hundreds. Still, it can be done. Most of us actually know more than a *thousand* people by name! What makes this possible is that we tend to group people by categories. There are people at work, neighbors, merchants you deal with on a regular basis, old classmates, historical figures, musicians, movie stars . . . and of course, family.

I come from a fairly large family and have over a hundred aunts, uncles, first cousins, second cousins, first cousins once removed, second cousins once removed, and so on. Andy, who claims that you can count his relatives on the fingers of one hand and still hitch a ride to the next town, was, needless to say, overwhelmed the first time he attended one of my family gatherings. After a couple of hours, he had to go off to a back bedroom, lie down, and take a few deep breaths.

Still, he quickly learned to know this assortment of individuals, and what helped the most was dividing them into subfamilies. The Kerrs are party animals and guaranteed to keep you laughing. The Allisons are

achievement-oriented and not burdened with false humility. The Cobbs are
Scotch. Actually, all the branches of my family are from Scottish ancestry,
but the Cobbs take frugality very seriously. If you get a note from a Cobb,
it will likely be written on scrap paper reclaimed from the wastebasket.

So—to help you sort native plants into less bewildering groups, I'd like
to introduce you to native plant families. A family is a grouping of plants.
All grasses, for instance, are in the Grass Family. Orchids are in the Orchid
Family. Lilies are in the Lily Family. There are dozens of plant families represented in North America, but three you'll meet over and over again
are the Rose Family, the Bean Family, and the Aster Family. If you can learn
these, you'll have taken a significant step in learning native American plants.

The Rose Family is characterized by white or pink flowers with five
petals. Unfortunately this doesn't mean that *every* flower with five petals is
in the rose family, and I know of at least one member of the Rose Family
that has four sepals and no petals (American burnet). Occasionally a rose
member will have yellow flowers, but this is quite rare. Most of the time,
if you see a flower with five white or pink petals, you'll be right if you
announce: "This is a member of the Rose Family."

I can see you frowning. You're thinking of hybrid tea roses with so
many petals it would make your head hurt to count them. Exempt hybrid
roses from your thoughts. Think of wild roses that need to have their sexy
centers highly visible so that bees will fertilize them and they can produce
rose hips. Think of the white cluster roses that sprout from the roots after
your hybrid rose has frozen to death. They all have five petals. All of them.

What else has five petals? Strawberry. Blackberry. Raspberry. Plum.
Cherry. Chokecherry. Juneberry, serviceberry, or shadblow. Hawthorn.
Crabapple. Apple. As you can see, a member of the Rose Family can be an
herb, a shrub, or even a tree. What groups these members of the Rose
Family together is that they have spring flowers with five petals, and they
have fruits that are brightly colored, pulpy, and full of vitamin C.

However, some members of the Rose Family have very different fruits.
Apache plume (*Fallugia paradoxa*) and prairie smoke (*Geum triflorum*)
are famous for their showy pink plumes of seed. Queen of the prairie
(*Filipendula rubra*)—an almost extinct branch of the family—and spiraeas
have tiny tan capsules. Their flowers may be large and single, or they may
be tiny and clustered, but they all have five white or pink petals.

The Bean Family is even more diverse, but if you see seeds encased in a
bean or pea pod, you're looking at a member of the Bean Family. Of
course, some members have beans so tiny, coiled, or clustered that you
don't recognize them as such. In that case, look at the flower. On the more
classic beans, the flowers are shaped like a head wearing a sunbonnet.

Sometimes they're big, like in sweetpeas and bluebonnets, and sometimes they're tiny and narrow and crammed into a spike like purple prairie clover (*Dalea purpurea*). A third clue is the leaves; they're divided into leaflets—often only three, but equally often one or two dozen arranged along a central spine. Another characteristic, one you can't see without a microscope, is that mycorrhizae on the roots help put nitrogen into the soil. That's why there'll be lots and lots of beans on nutrient-poor sandy soil.

Members of the Bean Family can include trees like mesquite, acacia, locust, and robinia, or they can be shrubs like leadplant (*Amorpha canescens*), or they can be herbs like Illinois bundleflower (*Desmanthus illonensis*) and bluebonnets (*Lupinus* spp.) and other lupines.

The Aster Family used to be called the Composite Family, and I like that a lot better. All daisies are members of the Aster Family. A daisy may look like one flower, but it is really a composite of a ring of ray flowers and a center of disk flowers. The ray flowers form the petals, and the disk flowers form the gold or green or dark brown center. Daisies are not just white. They can also be colored yellow, pink, purple, orange, or maroon. Sunflowers, Mexican hat, Indian blanket, zinnias, purple coneflower, and asters are all daisies.

Then, there are members of the Aster Family that are not so easy to identify. There are those with only ray flowers, like dandelions and chicory. There are those with only disk flowers, like thistles and gayfeathers (*Liatris* spp.). There are those where the flowers are clustered into big heads like yarrow. There are even some, like artemisia, with flowers so tiny and inconspicuous that you'll be surprised to learn they are kin to daisies.

But when you see a daisy, you can impress your friends and state with authority, 'That's a member of the Aster Family!'"

~

Our Unsung
Horticultural Heroes

~

Sally

True or false: It's a lot easier these days to find native plants in nurseries.

The answer is true. Before the mid-1980s, your average nursery carried only a few native shade trees; that was about all. By the 1990s, many of these same nurseries had at least a small sampling of native perennials, shrubs, ornamental trees, and even groundcovers. But the really big news is that today there is a growing list of specialty nurseries in most states that devote at least half of their stock to a wide selection of native plants.

This expansion of native nurseries is happening because public demand is increasing. But it's also occurring because now there are a large number of commercial wholesale growers willing to take on the challenges and problems inherent in entering this new industry on the ground floor.

That anyone gets into this business in the first place is remarkable. There may be tougher ways to make a living, but I'd be hard pressed to list many. The successful native plant grower must have, in equal measure, the botanical skills of Asa Gray, the green thumb of Luther Burbank, the financial acumen of J. P. Morgan, and the mind-reading skills of the Amazing Kreskin.

Before the mid-1980s, most of our nursery stock was nonnative and it was grown in California, Louisiana, and Tennessee. The grower purchased seed and cuttings that had gone through an extensive selection process; sometimes this involved hand-pollinated breeding or hybridization. And, the main thing we must understand is that, almost always, these selections had taken place in Japanese or European test fields where the climates and soils differ greatly from most parts of our country. This is why nurseries did such a good business replacing plants that died in our late freezes and summer dry spells.

Since the mid-1990s, a transformation in the nursery plant palette has taken place. A handful of individuals have contributed much to this evolution. A few that Andy and I are aware of are Tom Dodd in Alabama, Benny Simpson in Texas, Judith Phillips in New Mexico, Ron Gass in Arizona, Bob Evans in southern California, Neil Diboll in Wisconsin, and Alan Wade in Minnesota.

To give you an idea of what these pioneers have faced, below is a short description of the processes of developing plants for the nursery trade. To simplify the story, all the specific examples are from growers we've talked to in the Southwest.

One component of developing new plants for the nursery trade is test plots. One of the best was at the Texas A&M facility in North Dallas. There, before his untimely death, research scientist Benny J. Simpson worked with native trees and shrubs and developed and released several selections: "White Storm," a pure white desert willow and "Dark Storm," a two-tone burgundy and rose one, "Mount Emory," a mountain sage (*Salvia regla*), and five cenizos (the Cloud series). Several more trees, shrubs, and perennials were in the works when he died, including a chocolate-scented mock orange.

These, and his many other selections, were based on almost twenty years of hard work. Simpson made several trips a year, combing the state for attractive plants. He tagged desirable plants when they were in bloom, fall color, or fruit. He made return trips to gather seed or to take cuttings at the optimum time of year. By reading and experimentation, he figured out how to coax the seeds to germinate and the cuttings to root.

Then, he planted the seedlings and rooted cuttings in test rows and watched them. It takes years of observation to winnow out those that have the most drought-resistance, cold-hardiness, and beauty. Another consideration is ease of propagation. A plant that grows quickly and easily from a cutting is best. A cutting will produce clones, plants that look exactly the same each time—a boon to landscapers. Quick and easy growth is important if the wholesale nursery grower hopes to make a profit and stay in business. Once a particular plant in the test plot is selected and named, it becomes available to growers, who can purchase cuttings from these selections for a nominal price and save themselves a lot of hassle.

Most states don't have this advantage. In Glendale, Arizona, Ron Gass, a wholesale nurseryman and owner of Mountain States Nursery, uses as many of Simpson's selections from the Chihuahuan Desert as are applicable for the Sonoran and Mojave deserts where he makes most of his sales. But, to offer a wide range of desert plants, Gass must scout and select and test just like Simpson does, but at his own expense.

The time alone involved in a process like this is staggering. Suppose you've decided to grow Eve's necklace (*Sophora affinis*). You have to schedule a trip in the spring to find a community of trees where the color is a rich, pretty pink, and locate the clusters that are exceptionally large and luscious, that will make six- to nine-inch-long necklaces of black-beaded seeds. Eve's necklace with short, dirty-white clusters and short necklaces is not going to capture the hearts of the buying public.

Then you have to schedule a return trip when the seeds are ripe. You have to be clairvoyant and you have to be able to afford that kind of travel expense. It's possible for a grower to take off the exact same weekend as the previous year and drive hundreds of miles for ripe seed—only to discover the seed ripened early or won't be ready for another two weeks. Weather varies each year, and so does the exact date of ripening.

Even when you have the seed, things don't always go well. One year, Mary Buchanan of Texas Star Gardens in Abilene planted hundreds of chinquapin oaks for the Texas market. Each morning, when she visited her greenhouse, there were fewer acorns. Were they rotting without a trace? No, squirrels had chewed a tiny hole in a corner of the greenhouse and were coming in for a midnight raid. Mary discovered the hole, closed it up, gathered more acorns, and tried again. Then, she discovered that she had a double crop. Chinquapin acorns were sprouting everywhere; the squirrels had planted them in the dirt floor, in pots of perennials, in pipes, even in an old shoe.

But squirrels are the least of your problems. Seed almost always has to be fumigated; even as you gather it, you are gathering countless insects that feast on those seeds and will continue to chomp away until you get rid of them.

Many seeds are not easy to germinate. They require cold, light, darkness, acid baths, or combinations of these treatments, and timing is important. Creosote (*Larrea tridentata*), the most important evergreen shrub of the southwestern deserts, was not used in cultivated landscapes until very recently because no one could figure out how to propagate it. Dr. Jimmy Tipton finally discovered the secret when he was at the Texas Agricultural Experiment Station in El Paso. In 1990, Ron Gass finally figured out how to germinate the seed in a way that made it possible for creosote to be grown *en masse* for the nursery trade. But coldenia (*Tiquilia greggii*), a delightful silver and purple shrub-flower of the deserts, is still unavailable because, as of this writing, no one has been able to crack its germination code.

The other major way to grow plants is from cuttings, and that, of course, is another can of worms. For the highest rate of success, you need a mist bench—a sophisticated system that recreates a humid, rain-forestlike environment for the cuttings.

This can be an expensive investment for a grower just starting out. Some flowers, like that charming bedding plant known as blackfoot daisy (*Melampodium leucanthum*), can't be grown commercially without a mist bench.

To be successful with cuttings, you also have to know whether green soft shoots or hard woody ones root best for each specific plant. If it's hardwood cuttings, do they respond more readily if taken in the summer? The fall? When the plant is dormant? Hormones can greatly affect rate of growth—but which ones, and how much? The variables seem endless.

Now, let's imagine that you've mastered all of these obstacles. Finally, your seed is sown in flats and is coming up, the cuttings are leafed out and putting on new growth and you're home free. You wish!

Now you have to figure out what kind of soil mix to use. Most retail nurseries water several times a day—far too much for a drought-tolerant plant. So, you pot the plant in a light, fast-draining soil mix so it won't rot before it gets to a customer.

Correct fertilization is another gray area for native plants. For the most part, they prefer less fertilizer than conventional plants, but each grower must discover for himself how much or how little to use to get maximum growth for the least cost.

After all of this, you still face the problem of educating the nurseries you want to sell to, most of whom have never heard of you or your natives. Their salespeople need to know what native plants they'll be selling, how to display them properly, and how to care for them. They also need to know precisely which natives are best for their area and how to intelligently answer questions from the buying public.

Ah, yes, there's the public. This part of the business will really test your mettle, as you try to anticipate what they will want next year. If you have a demand for Turk's cap (*Malvaviscus arboreus* var. *drummondii*) this year and sell all that you can grow, you may not be able to give it away next year. Conversely, landscape designers and architects want to specify native plants of certain sizes and quantities on a landscape plan, and they don't know from one year to the next what will be available.

As more and more adventurous gardeners and landscape designers buy native plants, the plants become familiar to the general public and mainstream retail nurseries. As the demand for particular native plants stabilizes, growers are able to produce quantities, sizes, and species more dependably.

The next time you go to buy a native plant, you'll have a better chance of finding what you want than you would have had a few years ago. Thanks to the perseverance and dedication of those noble, unsung botanical heroes and heroines, the commercial native-plant growers, most gardeners can now choose from dozens of plants native to your area. But also thank your neighbors and yourself for being smart enough to buy native plants. It takes all of us working together to create a new industry.

PART V

Observations

I went to the woods because I wished to
live deliberately, to front only the essential
facts of life, and see if I could not learn what
it had to teach, and not, when I came to die,
discover that I had not lived.

—HENRY THOREAU,
Walden

∽

Rediscovering Our Lost Native Herbs

∽

Sally

How many native North American herbs can you name? If you know more than two, congratulations; even expert herbalists have trouble in this area. European and Asian herbs are far better-known. We simply have no idea how many native culinary and medicinal herbs we have. Much of this knowledge—the culmination of millennia of exploration and experimentation—has been lost along with our Native American cultures. Today, there are still a few medicine men and women who can relate herbal lore that was orally handed down to them, but even that is scattered and fragmented.

Herbs have been an integral part of humanity since prehistoric times. Oregano was discovered by anthropologists in European interglacial human deposits that were 160,000 years old. Ancient Greeks, Romans, and Egyptians used herbs extensively, such as parsley, rosemary, thyme, sage, marjoram, coriander (cilantro), dill, and garlic. And, cumin is mentioned in the Bible.

Ancient Mediterranean people defined "herb" more loosely than we do today. Along with perennials, they considered trees and grasses to be herbs, as long as the bark, leaves, flowers, roots, or fruits could be used for medicines, flavorings, teas, or fragrances. For example, they considered roses to be important herbs and used them as salve, perfume, and flavoring in puddings—and as a cure for hangovers. Their traditions are still our traditions. Today, we use rose water for flavoring foods, attar of roses for perfumes, and rose hips for teas. In fact, modern medicine employs rose hips in many of our prescription drugs.

Because much of our culture is derived from Europe, it's only natural that these European herbs are the ones we're most familiar with; our spice racks and grocery shelves, not surprisingly, reflect the predominance of Mediterranean herbs. The same is true of our typical herb gardens.

If you'd like your herb garden and your spice rack to go beyond the typical, then I suggest you take a look at some of our own native—and underutilized—herbs.

The current trend in herb gardening is the emphasis on the culinary, rather than the medicinal, properties of herbs. The aesthetic appeal of the herb garden is also becoming more important. It not only has to be useful and emit the spicy scent of aromatic leaves, today's herb garden must also have eye appeal.

The native herbs I will describe for you here meet all of the above requirements. Like Mediterranean herbs, they require good drainage, so plant them in a sloping bed, or in a well-prepared, raised bed.

Herb leaves contain pungent oil glands as a chemical defense against insects and vertebrate herbivores. Water sparingly for a more pungent flavor; a dryish soil causes the leaves to possess a higher proportion of aromatic oil.

You may find that some of our herbs are more drought-tolerant than Mediterranean herbs. Most of the United States has higher temperatures and longer periods of high evaporation. If you have been consistently losing a traditional herb in a particularly hot, sunny spot, try a native American herb. Here are a few I like:

Salvia. *Use the leaves in stuffings, salad oils, soups, cheeses, or in potpourris. Flowers are good in salads or for garnish.*

Salvia is the official botanical name for sage. The one you're probably familiar with is *Salvia officinalis*, the Mediterranean purple-flowered sage that has been used in Western medicine and cooking for thousands of years. Our native salvias, found mostly in the Southwest, have a similar flavor.

I find that the palatability of the leaves varies considerably during the summer, so always taste-test before you use salvia. From my own personal leaf-tasting sessions, I find that the red-flowered salvias are usually very nicely flavored, while the blue ones, although pleasantly aromatic, tend to be bitter.

My favorite red salvias for culinary purposes are autumn sage (*Salvia greggii*), mountain sage (*Salvia regla*), scarlet sage (*Salvia coccinea*), and cedar sage *(Salvia roemeriana)*.

All salvias are attractive garden plants as well as herbs. Most tend to bloom during the entire warm season, but peak bloom time for many is in late summer and early fall, when hummingbirds migrate.

Don't get these sages mixed up with the silver-leafed desert sages; sand sage, wormwood, and sagebrush are all artemisias. They have a wonderful aromatic smell but taste very strong and bitter, and more than one leaf can overpower and ruin any culinary effort. "Texas sage" usually refers to cenizo (*Leucophyllum* spp.), still another silver-leafed "sage," that seems to have some medicinal properties but is *not* recommended for cooking.

Monarda. *Use leaves as seasoning, in teas, or for garnish. Use flowers in sauces or for garnish.*

Bergamot (*Monarda fistulosa*) is a perennial that spreads by the roots. In winter, it is a four-inch-high mat of mint-fragrant leaves. By late spring, when it starts blooming, it is one and one-half to four feet tall, depending on how rich and deep your soil is and how much moisture it gets. Because it loses its root-shading rosette leaves, it needs good mulch in the summer to keep it from going dormant. With afternoon shade and watering, it might bloom all summer. The flowers are pale pink to pale lavender and smell as minty as the leaves. This plant was originally native primarily to the tallgrass prairie region, but it is grown in gardens all over the country.

The Rocky Mountain version of this mint (*M. fistulosa* var. *menthaefolia*) has a different flavor and is often called wild oregano. It can be used instead of grocery store (Greek) oregano. The herbalist Michael Moore, in his excellent book, *Medicinal Plants of the Mountain West*, recommends the spicy flowers for chili dishes.

The similar-looking red bergamot (*Monarda didyma*), called beebalm or Oswego tea, is native to the Appalachian Mountains, and is used widely in gardens where the summers are not too hot and dry. It's always a favorite with hummingbirds and butterflies.

Limoncillo. *Use in teas (good for colds), as a seasoning, or as a garnish.*

Limoncillo (*Pectis angustifolia*) is a charming, low-growing Western annual, native from Nebraska west to the eastern side of the Rockies, up to about 10,000 feet in Colorado, and south to Texas and Mexico.

It prefers sandy or rocky soils. Plant the seed in fall or in spring, after the danger of frost has passed. Starting in summer, the lemon-scented leaves will be covered with tiny golden-yellow daisies. Limoncillo is visually used to its best effect if allowed to drape itself over a wall, over the edge of a patio pot, or between stepping stones.

Chili piquin. *Use as you would jalapeños.*

Chili piquin (*Capsicum frutescens*) is also called bird pepper because the tiny ripe red peppers are very popular with birds. This is the original chili pepper, native from Arizona to southern Florida and throughout tropical America. Where temperatures rarely dip below freezing, chili piquin is an evergreen shrub that bears flowers and chilis most of the year. Further north, it might freeze back to the roots or reseed as an annual. It thrives in dappled shade.

Licorice. *Chew on naturally sweet roots, raw or dried. Can also be used as a tea.*

Licorice (*Glycyrrhiza lepidota*) is close kin to *Glycyrrhiza glabra*, the Zone 9 Mediterranean herb used to flavor licorice candy and cough syrups. Ours is far more cold-tolerant, native all over the American West from British Columbia to Mexico. It is found mostly in sandy arroyos and roadside ditches. The plant is rather pretty, usually about two feet tall, with spikes of creamy blossoms followed by velcro-textured pea pods. The leaves are light green and compound, a characteristic typical of the bean family.

This perennial goes dormant at frost, the best time to dig the roots. Don't worry about digging up your whole plant; it suckers like mad. Harvesting copious amounts of the roots each year is the only way to control it in the garden. Dig down at least eighteen inches to get to the best roots. Be sure to plant it in the sand it likes; then digging up huge portions of it each autumn will not become a formidable job.

Besides culinary seasoning, native herbs were used for medicines, and of course for food. A good book on Native American ethnobotany will also describe plants used for dyes, weapons, houses, horse medicines, and rituals. I have been extremely conservative on this list for culinary use, as Native American dishes may taste rather strange to modern palates. Everything here, however, I have tasted myself, with the exception of the licorice, which I abhor!

For further reading, here are some books I've especially enjoyed. *Uses of Plants by the Indians of the Missouri River Region* by Melvin R. Gilmore is my favorite because it is the oldest. It quotes information from nineteenth-century scouts, ancient medicine men, and the journals of explorers. Two books by Kelly Kindscher—*Edible Wild Plants of the Prairie* and *Medicinal Wild Plants of the Prairie*—combine these esoteric details with modern pharmacology. Some of the best descriptions for correctly identifying plants and brewing medicines are in *Medicinal Plants of the Mountain West* and *Medicinal Plants of the Desert and Canyon West* by Michael Moore. Two fascinating books on present practices are *Wild Plants of the Pueblo Province* and *Wild Plants and Native Peoples of the Four Corners* by William W. Dunmire and Gail D. Tierney.

"Just like that movie said . . . If you build it, they will come!"

~

Watch the Birdies
Instead of the Soaps

~

Sally

Back when Andy and I were first working on this book, a friend suggested that we include a chapter advocating bird gardens for retire-
ment homes. She'd installed one at her mother's nursing home and
had been amazed by how important the garden had become for many of
the other residents. For the bedridden, bird-watching out their windows
offered an exciting and refreshing change of pace from the intellectual stim-
uli of "Jeopardy" and "Days of Our Lives." And the more hardy and ambu-
latory elders actually enjoyed helping out with some of the upkeep chores.

At this point I should mention, for the benefit of sympathetic but
cost-conscious administrators, attracting birds is relatively simple and
inexpensive. We're not talking about the kind of sophisticated aviaries
you find in big city zoos. Install a birdbath. Water is essential for all creatures. To attract hummingbirds in the summer, simply hang out a few
hummingbird feeders and keep them topped off with sugar water (see
chapter 33, "Fast Food Stops for Hummingbirds"). For the winter, put

out a squirrel-proof sunflower seed dispenser and a feeder of smaller seeds. However, feeders like these tend to attract greedy English sparrows and starlings, so to get nesting songbirds and an interesting assortment of native migratory birds, you'll have to plant a few carefully chosen native plants— the flora our feathered friends are genetically programmed to look for.

Creating a Simple Bird Garden

- Select a spot fairly close to and easily visible from a main sitting area, such as a communal sitting porch, or outside the picture window of a dining or community room. A courtyard surrounded by many bedrooms with big windows is also effective.
- Mark off an "island" of at least thirty feet by fifteen feet. This will be the bird garden.
- Either clear the island of lawn grasses or stop treating it as a lawn. (It's not that grass is bad for the bird garden; in nature, trees and flowers grow in grassy meadows. But we want to set aside a space free of lawn poisons and mowers.)
- Outline its edges with a simple, unmortared stone wall, two stones high *or* create a wickerlike wall of sticks and branches left over from pruning. Either setting provides an environment for little insects and lizards, as well as other small creatures. These are summer snacks for the birds and, without them, the birds will be less likely to appear or stay around.
- This point is very important: Do not—I repeat, do not—use any poisons in this garden; you'll end up poisoning the birds that you're trying to feed.
- Now for the plants. Choose only those with similar water requirements. And those native to your area. (In the desert southwest, use cholla, prickly pear, mesquite, paloverde, acacia, cenizo, and creosote instead of the species listed below.)

    Choose one flowering tree. The flowers attract protein-rich insects at nesting time. By fall migration, the flowers have matured into small carbohydrate-rich fruits. Some trees that fit this scenario are various species of hawthorn, viburnum, amelanchier, chokecherry, our native flowering dogwood, or redbud.

    Choose a tree that produces dry mealy fruits that can survive winter weather. Holly species are especially good, but other candidates are alder, wax myrtle, sumac, and juniper.

Choose one evergreen and one dense thorny shrub for nesting and protection from weather and predators. If you've already chosen an evergreen holly, wax myrtle, juniper, or thorny hawthorn, you'll need only one more plant to fill this category. Some good choices that also produce berries are gooseberry, blackberry, and wild rose. (Don't worry if they fill the whole lower layer in the island. The birds will love it.)

As groundcover (if you didn't opt for berry bushes), plant a tiny meadow of unmown seed-bearing grasses. Some bird favorites are sideoats grama, fowl mannagrass, and inland seaoats. Add plenty of flowers. Daisy-shaped flowers attract butterflies, and tubular ones attract hummingbirds.

- Out in the open (away from the island and any trees) but in easy view, place a birdbath. It is important for the birdbath to be in an open space so cats and other predators can't hide within pouncing range.

Maintenance is easy; some of the more sprightly senior citizens should be able to do it themselves. In fact, I wouldn't be surprised if being on the bird-garden crew doesn't become a mark of distinction, sort of like being the blackboard monitor back in grade school.

The duties involved are simple and require very little effort: Fill the bird bath every day and make sure it's clean. Pull out ugly weeds and grasses that could overtake the pretty flowers and selected grasses. And, again, keep the hired maintenance crews from using any poisons on the plants in the island. If a maintenance person is spotted approaching with a spray bottle of toxic weed killer or insecticide, I'm told a cane waving in the air can be a marvelous deterrent.

"The party's at the Brinkleys.
Their possumhaws are fermented!"

32

∾

Things That Go
Bump in the Spring

∾

Sally

Every spring, back when we lived in Dallas, we'd hear a very unpleas-
ant sound—a loud thud against a windowpane. Not once, by the way,
but several times a week for at least a month. We'd cringe, knowing
what that sound meant, and we'd rush outside. There, sprawled beneath
the window would be a cedar waxwing, a bird easily identified by its soft
pale yellow belly, black mask, crest, and distinctive yellow band on the end
of the tail. There's also a small red waxy tip on each wing, which accounts
for its name.

The bird would not be dead, merely knocked senseless after flying full-
tilt into the window. Usually, the bird needed only a few minutes to pull
itself together. We gave it that chance, rounding up our cats and putting
them in the house, while our daughter Sora would stand guard over the
dazed bird until it could fly off again.

We used to speculate on why this happened so often and so predictably.
Did these waxwings flunk navigation in flight school? Were they simply

mentally deficient? Did they have poor eyesight? The answer is . . . they
were pickled! Looped! Soused!

Twice each year these waxwings fly through north central Texas. In the
fall, they escape the coming cold and travel to their winter vacation spots
down south—true "snow birds." Heading south, they are a sober lot. But
in the spring, on their way back north to their nesting sites, they turn into
rambunctious party animals. One last fling before beginning the serious
business of raising families, I guess.

And, where does the party begin? At the nearest possumhaw—the fruits
have fermented nicely over the winter, and the waxwings know it.

The possumhaw (*Ilex decidua*) is a fifteen- or twenty-foot multitrunked
holly tree that looks very much like the yaupon holly in the summer.
However, in the winter it sheds its leaves, leaving the female loaded with
colorful red to yellow fruit. The lack of leaves makes it much showier than
the closely related female yaupon.

The fruits ripen just as winter migration begins, but only a few get
eaten at this time. One theory suggests that birds rank fresh possumhaw
berries fairly low on their list of favorite nibbles; they'll dine on them only
when tastier treats are unavailable.

Personally, I favor another theory: these waxwings are no dummies.
They know that possumhaw berries, unlike other fruits that drop off before
spring, will last through the winter. So, they leave them uneaten, waiting
for the freeze and thaw cycles of winter to produce a fermented feast for
their spring bacchanal.

As winter storms blow and temperatures drop to startling depths,
Burford holly berries turn black; sometimes even the yaupon's are ruined.
But, the possumhaw fruits are still bright. This makes it a boon to garden-
ers looking for winter color.

If you live in Zones 6b to 9, and you'd like to plant a possumhaw in
your garden, make sure you get a female tree; females have all of the fruit—
although rarely you will run across a male with a few berries. Males are
essential for fertilizing the female; without at least one male in the immediate vicinity, the female will not bear fruit. Select your possumhaw in late
fall. That's the time of year when the berries are fully out and in good color,
and you'll know exactly what you're getting.

Then, choose a sunny site that is easily visible from the house or the
driveway. Those gaudy red berries glowing all over the tree make a heart-
warming sight on a gray winter day. And they are a welcome sight to
waxwings heading north in March.

33

∽

Fast Food Stops
for Hummingbirds

∽

Sally

Fall is the time of year when hummingbirds start heading south, flying close to the ground at speeds of up to sixty miles per hour. Hummingbirds are voracious feeders and fly low because they need to refuel their tiny bodies so often.

How voracious are they? Well, one study I read is extremely vivid. It compared the calorie consumption of an average-sized man—around 3,500 calories a day—to a hypothetical hummingbird of the *same* size. That hummer would require 155,000 calories a day. Another way to look at it is this: If you gave that man the same metabolism as the hummingbird, he'd have to eat 370 pounds of boiled potatoes each day to keep going. No wonder hummingbirds always have an eye peeled for snacks along the way. Kind of like going on a trip with a car full of kids.

People who live where summers are relatively cool get to enjoy hummingbirds all spring and summer; folks who live where winters are frost-free get to enjoy them all winter. The rest of us get to see them passing through, en route to and from their northern nesting grounds. By the end of September, they're usually getting ready to fly south on their annual fall migration to Mexico and Central America. And, instead of looking for golden arches along their route, they look for red plastic feeders hanging from tree limbs and porch eaves, filled with sugar water—junk food for hummingbirds.

In many ways, these feeders must be replacing the lost forage of native flowers, as hummers are the only native birds whose numbers are increasing.

However, there is no real replacement for flowers. When given the choice between sugar water and the sweet nectar of a fresh blooming flower—and I have friends who have experimented with this—a reasonably sane hummingbird will head for the nectar. Why? I used to think it must be vitamins and trace minerals, and maybe that is part of it. But it's been recently discovered that another attraction is tiny insects trapped in the nectar. It seems hummingbirds use sweets the way a runner does—for quick energy. The real food is insect protein. In the spring, when few hummingbird flowers are out, you'll see hummers around tree sap—another source of sugar and insects.

The flowers that attract hummingbirds are all colorful, ranging from vivid reds to golden yellows to vibrant blues. The favored blooms tend to be tubular or trumpet-shaped, the length of a hummingbird's tongue, which is about one and a half to two inches. And, although a number of imported blooms, such as eucalyptus and orange trees, attract hummingbirds, native flowers are the big favorites. This is not surprising, because these are the flowers that hummingbirds have evolved with. Hummingbirds are endemic to the Americas.

Some hummingbird favorites I can personally recommend are Turk's cap (*Malvaviscus arboreus* var. *Drummondii*), sages (*Salvia* spp.), trumpet vine (*Campsis radicans*), coral honeysuckle (*Lonicera sempervirens*), paintbrushes (*Castilleja* spp.), penstemons (*Penstemon* spp.), chuparosa (*Justicia californica*), anisacanthus (*Anisacanthus* spp.), gilia (*Ipomopsis* spp.), and coralbean (*Erythrina herbaceae*).

Each of these handsome flowers or vines has many reasons for being an asset to a home landscape, but I'd plant them just for the pleasure of looking out the window and spotting hummingbirds as they pause in midair while they stick their long, slender beaks into the flowers and suck out the nectar. Their body feathers are sleek and shiny, and the wings are beating so fast they are virtually invisible.

To make a hummingbird garden, choose a small area where the flowers will be massed very closely together. You will want to make a big splash of color so the hummingbirds can find you. Ideally, you'll want a full day of sun on your garden, although half a day is enough to get good blooms.

By the way, I heartily recommend Mathew Tekulsky's *The Hummingbird Garden* (Crown Publishers, Inc.). It's everything you've ever wanted to know about hummingbirds—and a lot you *didn't know* you wanted to know. This illustrated book is devoted entirely to the many fascinating and beautiful varieties of hummingbirds, how they live, how they behave, and how you can attract them to your property.

Goldenrod Is
Nothing to Sneeze At

Sally

Depending on your point of view, if you come across a field of goldenrod (*Solidago*) waving gently in the fall breeze, you'll do one of two things: reach for your camera—or reach for a handkerchief!

Many people think of goldenrod as "that blankety-blank plant that causes hay fever." Not true! This is a scurrilous, unfounded charge. Hay fever is caused by airborne pollens (not to mention airborne pollutants, but that's another soapbox).

Don't believe me? Okay, let's review some of that birds-and-bees stuff we all learned back in kindergarten: All flowers produce pollen to fertilize other flowers of the same species. A fertilized flower then produces seeds, and another generation is on its way.

Sex by long distance is not all that easy, however, so flowering plants have devised a number of ways to bridge the gap. Air pollination is the most ancient. The basic idea is to get so much pollen into the breezes that a sufficient quantity cannot fail to fall on flowers of the right sex and the right species. When you think about just how *much* pollen it takes to do the job, well, no wonder you get hayfever.

But, there's another way plants get pollinated. Bees, butterflies, and hummingbirds carry pollen. And, if you've ever watched them do it, you may have noticed that they generally head for the biggest, brightest, and sweetest-smelling blooms.

Examine the flower of a goldenrod closely. You'll find that there are actually hundreds of tiny flowers clustered together to make the very showy head. There is also a faint but pleasant fragrance. Now, do you hear a faint humming? That's the sound of bees. There might be several bees on each head of flowers. The bees are covered with the heavy sticky pollen, and, as they fly from one flower to another, they are transferring pollen, thus fertilizing the flowers.

The point is, goldenrod is *bee*-pollinated, not wind-pollinated. So, when you start sneezing, look around for the real culprit: ragweed. Ragweed is wind-pollinated, has an insignificant bloom, and is very common in every way.

Ragweed (*Ambrosia*) can have large leaves on thick green stalks that tower over your head, or it can grow only about knee-high and have grayish, narrowly divided leaves. The tall ones are found in seasonally moist or shaded grounds. You will find the small ones where it is very rocky or dry. Sometimes the two kinds can be seen growing just a few yards apart. They are most frequently found in disturbed ground that has been abused and prevented from developing its more civilized climax vegetation.

I often see the giant ragweed along creeks in the backyards of fancy suburban homes or in parks. There are many kinds of smaller ragweed, and they are usually found on bluffs and unmown vacant lots or in semi-abandoned pastures.

Ragweed is an annual and very easy to pull out. Once you learn to recognize it, you can pull it up in the spring, long before it ever thinks about blooming. If you pull it up while the goldenrod is blossoming, you can prevent some seed from ripening and dropping to the ground to start next year's crop. However, you probably can't pull ragweed out of every disturbed field for miles around, and its light smooth pollen is designed to travel for miles.

In our new home in Taos, New Mexico, artemisias, not ambrosias, are the culprits, while chamisa (*Ericameria nauseosa*) is the golden yellow beauty that gets unjustly accused. However, the artemisias are not weeds that can be pulled out. They're the cornerstone of sage scrub, a giant prairie-shrub system that extends northward and westward between the Rocky, Sierra Nevada, and Cascade Mountains all the way up into southwestern Canada.

Solution: In August, while buying a couple of fresh boxes of tissues, enjoy all the bright yellow flowers. Even bring them into your house in bouquets. They're not to blame.

≈

Trash Trees:
Mother Nature's Band-Aids

≈

Sally

Think of all the trash trees you wouldn't plant on a bet—the ones that get planted for you anyway by birds, wind, or squirrels. That list will include: mimosa (*Albrizzia Julibrissin*), tree of heaven (*Ailanthus altissima*), and chinaberry (*Melia azedarach*)—all nonnatives that have naturalized in various parts of the country. Then, there are the ones gardeners still love and nurseries still sell: Russian olive (*Elaeagnus angustifolius*), salt cedar (*Tamarix* spp.), Australian blue gum (*Eucalyptus globulus*), Chinese tallow (*Sapium sebiferum*), Norway maple (*Acer platanoides*), and white mulberry (*Morus alba*). Add to the list natives such as bristly locust (*Robinia hispida*), silver maple (*Acer saccharinum*), boxelder (*Acer negundo*), toothache tree (*Zanthoxylum americanum*), and hackberry (*Celtis laevigata*).

These are the weeds of the tree world, growing so fast that their wood is weak. Most of them mature and die in about thirty years, and their last ten years of life are usually painful to watch. They generally look pretty messy most of the time, continually dropping litter and seeds. Naturally, these trees are as prolific as rabbits. Every seed seems to sprout, and every sprout seems to live. And they're happy just about anywhere; no soil is too compacted, too wet, or too sunny. They'd really love to put down roots in your yard.

You can look at it two ways: These trash trees are either very adaptable or they have very low standards.

Why did Mother Nature give us trash trees? Because without them, many trees of higher quality couldn't get established.

This is how it works: Nature, as we learned in high school physics, abhors a vacuum. So, when a flood, landslide, or tornado has wrecked all of the existing vegetation and the soil is in danger of erosion, these spring-up-anywhere trash trees—along with weeds of the rankest description—become botanical "band-aids."

Their roots hold the soil, and their droppings become humus, giving better quality plants a chance to get established. Their thirty-year lifespan is the right amount of time to get a woodland going again. By the time the trash trees begin to die, young shade trees are outgrowing them, under-story trees are producing fruit, groundcovers are able to find enough leaf mulch to gain a foothold, and a fledgling woods is beginning to provide habitat for a rich array of plants and animals.

The trouble is that, years ago, way back before we got so smart, we actually imported trash trees from all over the world. They were highly touted by garden writers (we don't always know what we're talking about!), promoted and sold by nurseries, enthusiastically bought by homeowners, and planted everywhere.

Along the Gulf Coast, the cycle continues with Chinese tallow. You don't have to look very hard to find people who will tell you how won-derful this tree is: healthy, fast-growing, and hard to kill, even in the hands of developers and first-time, inexperienced homeowners. It has great red fall color, even in environments too warm for most trees to color. The white fruits of the female are decorative all winter and attract birds. Sounds like a winner, right?

Not according to what we're hearing from environmentalists, bird-watchers, and botanists: Chinese tallow is an environmental disaster. Like the beautiful but infamous flower *Lythrum salicaria* in the Northeast and several species of tamarix in the West, Chinese tallow is overrunning our wetlands. It is choking out the native vegetation that supports our wildlife. Wherever cuts are made for roadwork, an area is cleared for utility lines, or a hurricane destroys vegetation, Chinese tallow rushes in to fill the void.

When this happens in China, the results are just as Mother Nature intended. Here, however, it's the wrong "band-aid." The insects, fungi, and rodents that control tallow seedlings in China don't live here. And we certainly wouldn't want to import them; that kind of response more often than not just creates new environmental headaches. Nutria and walking catfish are examples that come instantly to mind. Here in the United States, the tallows establish themselves too thickly, and the oaks, maples, sweet-gums, wax myrtles, and other native vegetation that should be populating our wetlands can't get a toehold. They get squeezed out because they are operating within the natural limits of their environment, programmed to prevent a population explosion; the tallow, however, is operating *without* its natural brakes.

Leslie Sauer, landscape architect and environmental restorationist in Philadelphia, recommends that Norway maple and other noxious species be banned from being planted in the Northeast. The maple releases a toxic substance into the soil that prevents other plants from growing. She told me of one place in the Northeast where the land was cleared to make way for a new road. Four years later, Norway maple and sycamore maple (another imported trash tree) were well established and had kept some *300* native species from returning.

In California, you see vast stands of Australian blue gum eucalyptus, with nothing but bare ground underneath. Not only does this tree displace native vegetation and reduce biodiversity, it's a terrible litterbug. It sheds vast amounts of bark, twigs, and leaves, which make it very difficult for understory plants to get established. This litter is also a fire hazard and has fueled some of the worst forest conflagrations in California's history.

I am sure that in 50,000 years nature would get this all sorted out. But, if we don't intervene right now, Chinese tallow, Norway maple, Australian blue gum, and other imported trash trees will significantly reduce the numbers of many of our native species—both plants and animals—and none of us really knows how far the domino effect will reach.

Jean Michel Cousteau gave a talk in which he spoke about the dangers of lost species. He made a wonderful analogy: A plane is flying along with a madman on board. The madman is taking out rivets and tossing them away. The plane continues to fly along until, inevitably, one rivet too many is removed . . . and the plane comes apart. Our earth resembles that plane. The rivets are our many animal and plant species, all mysteriously and marvelously working in harmony to keep us aloft.

We are losing rivets all over the United States, and alien trash trees are one reason why. One year, when Andy and I were driving from

Connecticut to Tennessee, we were horrified by the amount of ailanthus deserts we saw—miles and miles of highway, lined with thickets of nothing but ailanthus. Woodlands of native oak, maple, and tulip poplar were sometimes seeding out right over them, but no seeds were able to penetrate down to the soil through those blankets of ailanthus. Not even smooth sumac (*Rhus glabra*), one of our most vigorous suckering native shrubs, a band-aid plant of the first order, was able to penetrate.

If we're going to save our natural heritage of native species, we're simply going to have to help out. If we want to turn raw, abused land back into a native, self-functioning woodland, it's going to be necessary for individuals, as well as environmentally oriented groups such as native plant societies, Boy and Girl Scout troops, and garden clubs, to step in and do some of Mother Nature's work for her.

First, get rid of those exotic trash trees. You don't have to use poisons to do it; some can be easily cut down. Others will sprout again, so you'll need to remove them by the roots. It's possible to uproot trees as large as six inches in caliper with an iron bar and a little muscle power.

Then, plant very small, container-grown oaks, elms, and understory trees in late fall, or while they are dormant in the winter. It's important to plant these trees in the right combinations and at the appropriate spacings. Observing uninvaded woodland of the same habitat near you is the best way to do this. Essentially, you've got to count species and try to duplicate the composition and spacing the best way you can. Then, gather up all of your neighbors' bagged leaves to use as mulch, and use biodegradable burlap to control erosion, if necessary.

Then, we have to hope that enough pieces of nature are still around to fill in the blanks. Because, the blunt truth of it is, as technologically sophisticated as we are, completely reconstructing a simple, natural habitat is no more possible than building a human body from scratch.

PART VI

Creating Habitats

People are so naive about plants, Ellie thought. They just chose plants for appearance, as they would choose a picture for the wall. It never occurred to them that plants were actually living things, busily performing all the living functions of respiration, ingestion, excretion, reproduction—and defense. People who imagined that life on earth consisted of animals moving against a green background seriously misunderstood what they were seeing. That green background was busily alive. Plants grew, moved, twisted, and turned, fighting for the sun; and they interacted continuously with animals.

—MICHAEL CRICHTON,
Jurassic Park

36

∼

How Natural Is Natural?

∼

Sally

There is a lot of talk these days about natural landscapes, and that's a big step in the right direction. But in many cases the type of landscapes being discussed aren't natural at all. A natural landscape, just so we're all on the same page, is the antithesis of the overly controlled environment found in a typical suburban yard.

I have read several fine books on the subject; they give directions on how to re-create woodlands and grass gardens and how to arrange a rocky stream to look like Mother Nature made it. So far, so good.

The illustrations in these books, however, tell a different story; these "slices of nature" are inhabited by plants from all over the world. And, while a few of them are able to sustain themselves, most would die without human intervention. In one book, the author mentions hundreds of natives in natural combinations, but then you get to the plans. Disappointingly, they call for the usual nursery selections, and that means, for the most part, ill-adapted aliens.

I belong to the school that believes a true natural landscape should be composed of only those plants that would have *naturally* occurred on that site. That means native plants—combined in the way that Mother Nature arranges them.

Today, many native plant lovers and environmentalists are taking this innovative and quite sensible point of view. When you think about it, this perspective has a lot of merit. For one thing, it's an extremely low-maintenance approach; the only water the plants need comes from normal rainfall (after being established, of course). One plant doesn't get in another's way because millennia have taught them how to grow together harmoniously. And, of course, there's the welcome bonus of small wildlife, such as butterflies, anoles, and fireflies, which add beauty and interest to the scene.

However, please don't misunderstand me; I'm not advocating a garden totally devoid of the guidance of the gardener. Annual pruning, shaping, weeding, and aesthetic adjustments are important even in a prairie or woodland reconstruction garden. A successful garden is a partnership between nature and the gardener.

"Natural" in its purest sense—how Mother Nature managed things before we started "helping" her out—just doesn't exist in North America anymore, and possibly hasn't since human beings arrived in the Americas. What Europeans saw as a completely wild landscape had been managed by Native Americans. They used fire to maximize habitat for deer, elk, and bison. In turn, vast herds of grazing and browsing animals also helped maintain savannas and prairies. By 1850, just as the climate changed from the Little Ice Age to the present warm-dry cycle, European land management practices eliminated fire and grazers and "harvested" the forests. Since the 1930s, even floods have been mitigated, changing, for example, the vast Colorado River cottonwood groves, willow banks, and sedge marshes from bird and fish habitat to irrigated farmland.

Obviously, there's just no way for us to return to the way it used to be when Native Americans were the stewards. We're not going to give up our farms, highways, factories, and shopping centers. And we certainly don't expect our population to reduce itself to the number of people who lived here when Columbus dropped anchor. (Although anthropologists currently estimate the numbers of Native Americans to have been vastly greater than what we used to think. There is evidence that diseases brought in by the Spanish sailors may have wiped out as many as 90 percent of some indigenous peoples.)

But, we *can* act to save what precious wilderness we still have. Europe has pretty much destroyed theirs. We, in the Americas, still have a chance to do better. All we need is some foresight, self-restraint, and common sense.

We can do something else, too. We can re-create our natural habitats in parklands, along highways, on the grounds of schools and businesses, and around our homes. They won't be *true* natural habitats, of course. In the strictest sense, re-creating a true natural habitat may not be possible, even in our vast national parks. Yellowstone, however, has been making a valiant attempt; it's building up a herd of bison and reintroducing natural predators. It will be interesting to see how it all works out.

But those of us who own a bit of land—and you really don't need acres and acres—can have a modified natural native landscape—a *naturalistic* landscape. An area no larger than a typical suburban lot is enough to re-create a miniprairie or woodland around your home.

Many people are astounded to hear that they can have a miniwoodland on their property. But, they'd probably agree that they have enough land to accommodate two, three, or four shade trees, along with a complement of understory trees and assorted native shrubs, vines, groundcovers, and wildflowers. Well folks, that *is* a woodland.

A prairie landscape is perhaps harder to imagine. You are probably picturing crumpled stalks of brown grass as seen on vacant lots. Let me assure you that this is not what you would be attempting to achieve. I've seen lovely prairie home landscapes that have an arc of tall prairie grasses, thick and lushly green in the summer, golden with tawny colors in the winter, and dancing with wildflowers in the spring. You can mow walkways through the tall grasses to reach open spaces such as lawns, patios, or decks. For trees and shrubs, use the ones that were found along local creeks or those that once naturally bordered the prairies. This combination of woodland and grassland is called a savanna, and it is the richest habitat of all. Flowers, fruits, and wildlife abound.

As for maintenance—if your grass is not being grazed by bison, land tortoises, or rabbits, you will have to mow once a year. If you don't have deer, elk, or moose to browse your shrubs and trees, you'll have to prune once a year. Tallgrass prairies thrive on fire, and while most homeowners flinch at the thought of a fire, it's possible to have a "cool burn" with trained neighbors and firemen beside you.

The truth of it is, wherever you live in the United States, there is a gorgeous natural habitat that you can adapt as a garden. The southern hardwood forest in Ohio, the rocky diversity of Idaho's grasslands, the Sonoran Desert in Arizona, or coastal sage scrub in San Diego, California—each can make a landscape worthy of being featured in any garden magazine. There is simply no end to the natural landscapes that America has to offer.

In order to maintain this precious natural history, we as gardeners can make a big difference. We can use our native plants in natural combinations, cleaned up just enough to suit our aesthetic tastes or to keep our fussy neighbors happy. In doing so, we do more than give ourselves an attractive, easy-care landscape. We help preserve our plants, their gene pools, and at least some of the animals that evolved along with them.

37

∾

Create Your Own Woods

∾

Sally

One of the smartest things I ever did was to select a mother who owned a good-sized piece of unspoiled woodland in east Texas. Our escapes to that serene haven of arboreal beauty and welcome quiet were far too infrequent.

Although, to be truthful, things weren't all that quiet there. Bluebirds called to each other and played among the branches. Rustling leaves revealed the presence of quail searching for food. And there was almost always a breeze—and a squirrel or two—stirring in the treetops. Nighttime was clamorous with tree frogs and chuck-will's-widows.

The woods were alive!

The bustle of our man-made world was shut out. We would sit motionless in the woods on some moss, under a friendly old tree, and feel like we were a million and one miles away from traffic snarls, shopping malls, newscasts, and junk mail.

The lure of the woods is strong; people will drive hundreds of miles to camp or picnic out in the wild. Nearly everyone would like to have a home nestled in such a setting. Many are even willing to pay extra to buy a homesite with lots of mature trees on or at least abutting it.

But many others live in suburban "bedroom" communities where developers have scraped and leveled, planted a few puny shrubs, sprinkled grass seed, and called it landscaping. How dull!

Surely a woods is out of the question for this kind of setting. . . .

Or is it?

I'm happy to report that you can undo that sterile suburban look the developers saddled you with. Virtually any home, as long as it's on land that can support trees (east of the 100th meridian or in mountains or alongside water), can have a more natural, woodsy landscape. And, if you can't, or aren't willing to give up the "athletic" field out front where Dad and Junior can toss the frisbee back and forth (By the way, when was the last time *that* happened?), then you can at least have a miniwoodland in one corner. Or in your backyard.

Aside from its obvious aesthetic appeal, there are many advantages to a woodland landscape. You don't have to water or fertilize once it has been established. There is no need for you to even own a lawnmower or hedge clippers. Maintenance becomes annual instead of weekly, and it consists of a once-a-year project that includes pruning, cleaning out deadwood, maintaining paths, and fighting the undesirables: poison ivy, to which some people are highly allergic (like me); greenbriar, which creates thorny impenetrable thickets; Japanese honeysuckle, which is evergreen and smells good when in bloom, but is overly enthusiastic; or whatever is rampant and unwelcome in your region. The battle against such plants is an ongoing engagement because birds love their berries and replant the seeds on a regular basis. Furthermore, the roots are formidable; they laugh at ordinary applications of poisons, assuming you'd be so environmentally incorrect as to use them. Control is more realistic than eradication.

In the spring, before the leaves come out, the woods will seem to float in dainty white and pink. In the summer, the foliage is thick and lush, making your neighbors often invisible. Traffic noises are softened. It's even cooler inside your wooded sanctuary; the drop in temperature as you enter your woods is dramatic. And consider how that will affect your air conditioning bills.

In the fall, there is another burst of color, red and gold this time, made more vivid by evergreens. Don't rake the leaves. As they turn brown, they will protect the little woods violets and other spring flowers and provide the fertilizer for next year's round of beauty.

In the winter, the woods are sleeping. But the woodland creatures are not. If you have a lot of berries and seeds, your woods will be raucous and colorful with birds wintering over.

Well, now that I have all of you absolutely panting for at least one part of your property to be a woodland, let me tell you how to make it that way. True, it won't resemble Sherwood Forest, but all of the basic components will be there for shade, beauty, and wildlife.

First, for those of you fortunate enough to already have woods on your land, you can enhance its beauty by adding the color of small flowering trees and groundcovers native to your immediate area. Just be sure the spot you pick out for the new plant's home is similar to where it grows naturally.

If there are open spaces in your woods, plant your additional color here. If your woods are already very thick, cut down a few saplings of your dominant species to create space enough for other varieties. Then, mark each open place with a stake. Sit in your favorite viewing spot and image a small flowering tree where each stake is planted. You'll probably have to rearrange the stakes several times before you are satisfied. This is much easier as a two-person job, with one to view and one to move the stakes.

After you have chosen which trees (shrubs, flowers, and so forth) to use, plant small ones so they can establish themselves easily without a lot of supplemental watering. Make notes on your calendar to check new plantings at two-week intervals during the summer. Check in the spring and fall as well if rainfall is below normal.

If you are on a developer's lot, scraped clean with no telling whose soil heaped on top, or an old established yard with no pizzazz, here is how to start your woods from scratch:

For every one hundred square feet of woods (10' × 10'), there is usually one large shade tree, four saplings, and seventeen shrubs or understory trees. This is a dense woods that will screen a view and show little or no ground. Do not plant this densely. Restrain yourself to one one-inch diameter shade tree, two understory trees, and two groundcover items such as low shrubs, ferns, flowers, or woodland sedges. These plants will either sucker or seed out, so by the time the shade tree is four inches in diameter, you will have a dense woods. Or you can keep the saplings thinned out and have an open and more colorful woods.

Do not plant anything in a straight line. Are you familiar with the trick of naturalizing bulbs? Take a sackful of bulbs, and toss them out on the ground. You plant them where they land. Plan your woods the same way, but on a vastly larger scale. Obviously, I don't expect you to fling trees and shrubs all over your yard, but you can throw bricks or stones or potatoes.

Begin by dividing your yard into ten- by ten-foot squares. This can be done with stakes or garden hoses or, in bare dirt, by making a groove with a hoe. Then, toss one brick into each square. At each brick, flag the spot for a shade tree and repeat the process for the flowering understory trees and for the groundcovers. If one of your shade tree bricks misses the intended square and ends up in another, don't throw it again. Plant the tree right there, and call it kismet.

If you need to create a visual barrier, plant evergreens or thicket-forming trees and shrubs in double strength on the offending boundaries.

Now you are ready to choose which plants to use. Notice, I said, *you*. There isn't room enough here for me to lay out the almost endless possibilities. Each area of the country has its own unique native woodland: pine woods, oak woods, maple woods, beech woods, fir-aspen woods, mesquite woods, and juniper woods, to name a few. Each also has its own palette of complementary understory trees and shrubs.

So you, dear reader, will have to do a little research among your own local native plant experts. There's very likely a native plant society in your state (most states have one) or a wildflower society. Or, you may be fortunate enough to have a local nursery where they know and carry native plants.

However you arrive at your own woodland plant list, be assured that it will work with the basic scheme I've outlined. But, you must make sure you are planning the correct woodland habitat for your site, or you lose all of those easy-care benefits.

With native plants, "a rose is a rose is a rose" will not work. If you live in gray oak country, red oak or live oak are not viable substitutes. You'd have to water forever to keep them alive and the understory shrubs and flowers would end up being a water dependent mishmash from all over the world—little better for water conservation, habitat, or your leisure time than a lawn.

But a native woodland is a year-round visual treat. In the summer, it is green and cool. In the spring, there are the lovely limes and peaches of budding leaves, and the white, pink, and blue blossoms of the understory trees and woodland wildflowers. In autumn, there are colorful fall foliage and ripe berries, and often red and yellow flowers. In winter, the majesty of the trunks soaring to the sky, the tracery of the branches (often red or purple with the promise of life held in check), and the thick carpet of decomposing leaves hold the scene in hushed suspense.

Of course, what's all that compared to a lawn and a box hedge?

~

Little Prairie by the House

~

Sally

When you hear the word "prairie," you probably picture a vast, seemingly limitless sea of tawny grass undulating to the horizon. There's not a single tree to be seen anywhere. Big sky country. If you've ever read true-life stories of the pioneers, diaries and other first-person accounts, you know that the sound of the wind blowing through the grass was so constant and so loud that some poor souls were literally driven mad by it. You also probably remember tales of settlers beating out rampaging prairie fires with wet blankets, hoping to save the house and barn, while wild animals thundered, grunted, bugled, and snorted by them, fleeing before the flames. And you remember the arcticlike blizzards from the *Little House on the Prairie* books and television series.

Is this what you can expect if you decide to re-create a prairie on your property? Relax. Unless your land measures in thousands of acres, those scenes I have just related are highly unlikely. Having a patch of prairie in your front yard is really not an off-the-wall idea. In its most basic sense, a prairie is just a tall lawn with flowers.

Our great western grasslands ended up being called prairies because the first Europeans to see them were French explorers who had come up the Mississippi River. "Prairie" is a French word that means "meadow," although it may be hard for us to equate the two terms. Settlers in New England called their grasslands meadows, and proceeded to tame them with fences. When the English-speaking pioneers ventured out west and saw those staggering stretches of grassland, it never occurred to them to call them meadows; it would have been like calling a whale a guppy. So, they conveniently forgot that the French word meant the same thing and adopted prairie into our vocabulary.

In broad stroke, all native landscapes are divided into grasslands and woodlands. Grasslands can be wet or dry. In poorly drained areas, they are called marshes. On uplands, they are known as prairies or meadows. Although, to get you thoroughly confused, I must tell you that many people in the South call marshes prairies as well. In this book, whenever I use the term prairie I mean grasslands of all sorts, as Mother Nature and Native Americans maintained them before we imported invasive species.

The most exciting landscapes in North America are found where grassland and woodland meet. Called savanna, this rich habitat is where the greatest number of plant species are gathered, as it combines grassland (sunny), woodland (shady), and savanna (half-sun–half-shade) species. Savanna is where you will find the variety, the color, and lots of wildlife. It's where the action is.

We humans seem to have two elemental drives that influence where we choose to live. We want homes that are sheltered by trees—perhaps a trait held over from our arboreal ancestors. We also have a need to surround ourselves with open spaces where it is safe to walk, where lions and tigers and bears can't sneak up on us.

We can accommodate both basic needs with a successful and satisfying prairie garden that combines savanna trees and shrubs with an open prairie area made accessible by a mowed walkway and perhaps a bit of lawn area. How your particular prairie looks will depend on where you live, what you plant there, and how you maintain it. Choosing plants that can grow on your site naturally, without any help from you, is the key to success. For the most part, you want to choose the grasses that would have been climax for your site. Not only will they be dependable and long-lived, but they are invariably among the prettiest, the best behaved, and the most nutritious for wildlife.

The largest contiguous prairie habitat was between the Mississippi River and the Rocky Mountains. East of the 100th meridian were tallgrass prairie and oak savannas. West of it were shortgrass prairie and juniper savannas. (Prairies and savannas are more than 99 percent extinct, so I tend to think of them in the past tense.) Other kinds of prairies were coastal prairies, the totally extinct Palouse Prairie in Idaho, the California intermontane prairies, desert grasslands, and odd patches of tallgrass prairies in New England and Appalachia or funky shortgrass prairies on limestone knobs in Tennessee.

In other words, wherever you live in North America, if you have sun, you can have some form of prairie, although some soils are better for trees. Most grasses prefer rich deep soil with a more alkaline pH. It's always interesting to drive north on the Natchez Trace Parkway in Mississippi; you pass a cypress swamp and immensely tall woods of sweetgum and oaks, with hydrangeas beneath—and then, all of a sudden, the trees become squat, and fields of grass and crops appear. What is happening here? The soil changes from acid sand to black clay loam, and just that quick you are out of the woods and onto the prairie.

This was prairie where the Chickasaw lived. Here the soil is rich enough to grow corn and other crops. There was once good forage for deer and elk with plenty of open space for bow-and-arrow hunting.

From early settlers' accounts, it seems that Long Island and much of Rhode Island were once similar prairies. These eastern prairies were less than waist high and were, essentially, islands in an ocean of forest.

Broomsedge (*Andropogon virginicus*) is usually the most common grass in an eastern prairie. Plant it with a vetch or clover and as many of these flowers as you can, choosing local species—fleabane (*Erigeron*), black-eyed Susan (*Rudbeckia*), milkweed (*Asclepius*), beebalm (*Monarda*), coneflower (*Echinacea*), and Joe-pye weed (*Eupatorium*). This mixture will get you started; you can add and refine as you go along.

In the Midwest, tallgrass prairies (sometimes taller than a man) were the dominant vegetation; trees were confined to the creeks. This land that grew lush grasses also grew lush crops (after all, corn and wheat are grasses, too), and very few prairie remnants were kept as hay meadows. Big bluestem (*Andropogon gerardii*), little bluestem (*Schizachyrium scoparius*), Indian grass (*Sorghastrum mutans*), and switchgrass (*Panicum virgatum*) are known as the "big four" of tallgrass prairie. These are the long-lived equivalents of oaks in a forest—the climax species—and they are a visual pleasure all year round. The fall and winter colors range from copper to gold; in the winter, the colors fade a bit but are still striking. Summer greens are rich and often bluish. Use switchgrass in the wetter sites and little bluestem where it is dry. North of the 39th parallel, add prairie dropseed (*Sporobolus heterolepis*) to your list. This knee-high, finely textured grass is greenish gold and makes, in my opinion, the prettiest prairie of all.

There are a myriad other grass species, many quite lovely, as well as an overwhelming number of prairie perennials (called forbs). One tiny prairie remnant in Waco, Texas, surrounded by city, was found to contain 20 species of grasses and 115 species of forbs. Twelve of these forbs are legumes (pea family), which are important nitrogen-fixers for the soil.

To start a tallgrass prairie, plan to begin with the big four grasses or prairie dropseed (if you live far enough north), and add these durable perennials in the Aster Family: coneflower (*Echinacea*), goldenrod (*Solidago*), aster (*Symphyotrichum*), sunflower (*Helianthus*), gayfeather (*Liatris*), ironweed (*Vernonia*), and rosinweed (*Silphium*).

Also, use at least two legumes: prairie clover (*Petalostemum*), clover (*Trifolium*), Illinois bundleflower (*Desmanthus illinoensis*), and milkvetch (*Astragalus,* which includes locoweed) are some of the most attractive and widespread.

To choose the actual species that would be native for you is important for your prairie to have health and longevity. I (immodestly) must admit that my *Gardening with Prairie Plants* (University of Minnesota Press) is an excellent guide to help you make the right choices.

Be aware, as you design your garden, that these flowers and grasses, with the exception of little bluestem and gayfeather, have stout aggressive root systems that can be kept in bounds only by pavement or weekly mowing during the growing season.

As you go further onto the Great Plains, the big four continue, especially little bluestem, but needlegrasses (formerly all *Stipa*) become increasingly important. Where it is really hot and dry, and rainfall averages ten to fifteen inches a year, the grasses get shorter, and the flowers become even more numerous. This is where you start getting spectacular spring colors. Buffalograss (*Buchloe dactyloides*) and blue grama (*Bouteloua gracilis*) are two of the most prevalent and desirable short grasses. Easy-to-purchase spring flowers include paintbrush (*Castilleja*), Indian blanket (*Gaillardia pulchella*), prairie verbena (*Verbena bipinnatifida*), penstemon (*Penstemon* spp.), and Tahoka daisy (*Machaeranthera tanacetifolia*).

In the desert grasslands that stretch from West Texas to Tucson, Arizona, a mixture of sideoats grama (*Bouteloua curtipendula*), plains bristlegrass (*Setaria macrostachya*), plains lovegrass (*Eragrostis intermedia*), and blue grama combine nicely for a soft, mid-shin look. Wildflowers might include paperflower (*Psilostrophe tagetina*) stemless evening primrose (*Oenothera caespitosa*), Colorado four-o'clock (*Mirabilis multiflora*), desert marigold (*Baileya multiradiata*), and phacelia (*Phacelia integrifolia* or *P. intermedia*).

West of the Rockies, the grasslands are broken up by mountain ranges; rainfall patterns differ significantly, creating a number of distinct prairies.

The southern California prairies near Los Angeles and San Francisco—usually called the valley grasslands—are probably the best known. The original grasses have been overgrazed and replaced by exotic annual species that give the famous golden summer color. But to start a real prairie, plant waist-high needlegrasses (*Nasella pulchra* and *Nasella cernua*), and the once ubiquitous soft-textured bluegrass *Poa scabrella*. Where temperatures often soar above 100°F, use two melic grasses (*Melica californica* and *Malica imperfecta*) with the needlegrasses.

Like the annual grasses, these original perennial prairie grasses will be green only from late October to late April. There are spectacular flowers to go with these grasses. The California poppy (*Eschscholtzia californica*) turns the hillsides golden in late February or early March. By April, it is joined by mariposa lily (*Calochortus*), lupine (*Lupinus*), owlclover (*Orthocarpus*), blue dicks (*Brodiaea*), baby blue eyes (*Nemophila*, especially *N. menziesii*), and gilia (*Gilia*).

The prairies of the Northwest are basically divided into moist prairies on the western side of the Pacific coastal ranges and dry ones on the eastern side. The coastal prairies are dry and dormant in the summer in northern California, but get considerably moister as you go north into Oregon. The most important grasses are the same. California oatgrass (*Dathonia californica*) is difficult from seed but essential. Blue wild rye (*Elymus glaucus*) tolerates some shade; use it where the prairie meets shrubs and trees. Red or molate fescue (*Festuca rubra*), a weeping bunchgrass with reddish flowers, doesn't become a dominant in California, but is so lovely you'll want to use it anyway. These are cool weather grasses, green in the spring, dormant in the summer where there is drought and in the winter where cold is severe. On especially moist sites, use tufted hairgrass (*Deschampsia caespitosa*) with its great heads of flowers that turn from green to red to gold.

On drier prairies, Idaho fescue (*Festuca idahoensis*) is a dominant, both in the northern California coastal prairie and on the intermontane prairies, where it is joined by bluebunch wheatgrass (*Agropyron spicatum*) and the slightly shade-tolerant prairie Junegrass (*Koeleria cristata*).

Flowers for all these Northwest prairies include blue dicks (*Brodiaea*), blue-eyed grass (*Sisyrinchium*), mariposa lily (*Calochortus*), lupine (*Lupinus*), clarkia (*Clarkia*), Oregon sunshine (*Eriophyllum lanatum*), shooting star (*Dodecatheon pulchellum*), rosy corn salad (*Plectritis*), the big-headed clover (*Trifolium macrocephalum*) and, in really wet places, camas (*Camassia quamash*). Be sure to use local species for long-term results.

You might opt to maintain your prairie the way Native Americans did; they used prairie fires as a necessary tool to keep brush and trees out, so the grasses wouldn't get shaded out. Mowing once a year is more manageable for most homeowners. One big advantage to a fire is that ash returns the nutrients to the soil. Using a mulching or flail mower that reduces stems and leaves to a fine-textured mulch and drops them back onto the soil is the next best treatment. Time of year is significant. A mow or fire in late summer seems to benefit butterflies and spring flowers, while a late-winter/early-spring cleanup benefits fall flowers.

Those with ranches might want to use grazing elk, pronghorn, deer, and buffalo as management tools. If you have horses, cattle, or sheep, try the Alan Savory rotation plan. I have seen and heard of many very impressive results with this method. The key is to have intense grazing but only for a week or so, giving the prairie months to recover. This mimics the bison herds that circled their territory once a year.

I hate to end on a negative note, but Mother Nature didn't have to weed out invasive species to start a prairie—there weren't any in those days. You will. Or else watch your efforts be overrun. Once your prairie is well-established and functioning as one harmonious, organic unit, it can keep most weeds out by itself but it will take a few years.

❧

A Kinder, Gentler Desert Garden

❧

Sally

What's wrong with this picture?: The groundcover is gravel or uniformly sized bits of colored rock, carefully kept clean and tidy with one of those outdoor vacuum cleaners or a leaf blower. Often, rocks of different hues, ranging from battleship gray to coral, are separated from each other by concrete scalloped edging. (Allowing them to mingle would be tacky.) Sometimes, the gravel is dyed green . . . to simulate a lawn? Occasionally real creativity is called into play, and you may find a stream of baby blue pebbles meandering beneath a miniature pink wrought-iron bridge.

Residing next to drip irrigation heads are cacti of various kinds, along with yuccas and other spiny succulent desert flora. Some homeowners, newly arrived from up north or back east, become smitten with this exotic flora and venture out into the desert to collect their own plants. They then proceed to cram as many as they can onto their properties, creating a confused mish-mash of "arms," "tongues," "spikes," and "daggers."

Or, they will go to the other extreme, placing a single plant here, another way over there, still another at the other end of the yard. Each is ringed with whitewashed river rocks. There is no cohesion here, no sense of flow, and no drama.

Underneath it all are impenetrable sheets of plastic weed barrier, holding down whatever "weeds" (whether exotic farm weeds or native plants) that may be lurking below, preventing dirt or sand from getting into the pristine gravel, keeping rain off the soil.

If you live between El Paso and Los Angeles, you've seen these desert gardens. They are everywhere. And they have absolutely nothing to do with the real desert.

For those of you in the Phoenix area, one vivid way to see how dramatically different the real desert looks is to visit Frank Lloyd Wright's Taliesin West in Scottsdale. To reach Taliesin West, you must first drive through miles of middle-class and upscale subdivisions. Here, you'll see those cactus and gravel landscapes in boundless variety. You'll also see another style of landscaping: lavish green lawns surrounded by luxuriant tropical plants. These, needless to say, get watered once or twice a day. The cactus/gravel style, at least, makes a concession to the climate and water shortages. But both are as inappropriate as giggling during High Mass.

Ah, but then you enter the road that takes you up to Taliesin West, and the Sonoran Desert surrounds you. This scene is far greener and softer than the gravel garden. The saguaros (*Carnegiea gigantea*) and palmillas (*Yucca elata*) are sensibly spaced apart, so that each can lay out a wide network of surface roots to catch even the merest hint of rainfall . . . sometimes as little as .01 of an inch. They are the trees of the desert landscape.

The groundcover is not gravel. While there is bare soil and rock showing on the desert floor, it is more than half covered with a variety of soft, nonspiny plants that pull the whole scene together. Here are bursage (*Ambrosia dumosa*), brittlebush (*Encelia farinosa*), and globe mallow (*Sphaeralcea ambigua*). Thornless, these knee-high plants have gray-green leaves. The brittlebush has bright yellow daisies in the spring, and the globe mallow blooms for a long time and has satiny blossoms in orange or pink.

Find an arroyo and you'll see another prime plant for those who live in the Sonoran Desert. Paloverde (*Parkinsonia* spp.) is a small tree, the perfect size for large or small gardens. Its lacy leaves and lime-green trunks are especially lovely next to a smooth adobe wall. When the whole tree turns orange-gold with spring flowers, it is nothing short of spectacular.

A shrub you ought not to pass up is pink fairyduster (*Calliandra eriophylla*). After every rain it bursts into a mass of pink fluffy flowers. It is particularly vivid when teamed up with that ever-blooming yellow daisy called desert marigold (*Baileya multiradiata*).

And don't forget the grasses. Most people are amazed to learn that a surprising diversity of native desert grasses once supported land tortoises, pronghorns, and other desert grazing animals. These grasses grow in clumps—not close enough together to make a sod. They make marvelous accents and backdrops, and their soft textures visually bind the desert together.

Sacaton (*Sporobolus wrightii*) used to be thick under the paloverdes or wherever the desert rivers flooded. Curly mesquite grass (*Hilaria belangeri*) grows at the base of the saguaros. Purple threeawn (*Aristida purpurea*) is one of the few native grasses readily available commercially for the low, hot deserts. When massed and in bloom, purple threeawn looks like a low pink cloud hovering over the ground. In true desert sand, plant golden knee-high drifts of the bunch grass big galleta (*Hilaria rigida*). For a very different feel, use bush muhly (*Muhlenbergia porteri*); its foot-tall wavy stems make it look like it just had a perm. Black grama (*Bouteloua eriopoda*) is more like a groundcover; it forms a wooly-white curly mat that is usually only about six inches tall. These grasses also work in the Chihuahuan and Mojave deserts.

The Chihuahuan Desert is as rich as the Sonoran Desert in beautiful nonthorny plants. Some of my favorite flowers are the rich purple trumpets of desert four o'clock (*Mirabilis multiflora*), the chocolate flower (*Berlandiera lyrata*), mesa greggia (*Nerisyrenia camporum*), and fragrant evening primrose (*Oenothera caespitosa*). Two lovely low-growing shrubs are trailing indigobush (*Dalea greggii*) with its purple flowers and the dazzling gold of turpentinebush (*Ericameria laricifolia*). For trees, I love the desert willow (*Chilopsis linearis*). This beautiful tree has long narrow willow-like leaves and it blooms off and on all year in shades of pink, lavender, white, or deep rose, or in two-tone combinations of these colors.

Some of the gentle flowers for the Mojave Desert are that huge yellow daisy Panamint daisy (*Enceliopsis covillei*), the vivid spring magenta of purple owls clover (*Castilleja exserta*), and desert Canterbury bells (*Phacelia campanularia*). For height, use Joshua tree (*Yucca brevifolia*) or the lime-green shade tree Torrey mesquite (*Prosopis glandulosa* var. *torreyana*).

For all these deserts use these two nonspiny shrubs—creosote (*Larrea tridentata*) and Apache plume (*Fallugia paradoxa*). Creosote, a large evergreen shrub with tiny dark green leaves and bright yellow flowers, is famous for that wonderful after-the-rain scent its leaves emit. Apache plume is almost ever-blooming and evergreen. It has white rose flowers that quickly turn into bunches of pink plumes that remain colorful for months.

By now, I hope you're creating a lovely desert landscape in your mind's eye: majestic cacti and dramatic yuccas, softened with shrubs, flowers, grasses, and lacy-leaved trees. . . . It provides a year-round color scheme of gray-green, blue-green, dark green, and lime-green with tawny grasses and bursts of vivid colors when the desert flowers bloom in the spring.

Drip irrigation goes with that traditional isolated-plant look I mentioned earlier; it doesn't work with the new and more natural desert look I've just described. Here a bubbler makes more sense. And not watering at all (once the plants have been established by watering with a hose for one to three years) makes even more sense. But that means you have to choose only those plants native to you, and you have to utilize every little drop of rain that falls on your land. Obviously, black plastic is a no-no; it doesn't allow the rain to soak into the ground. To keep whatever rain falls on your property, use swales. Catch the runoff from the roof, the patio, and any paved walks or driveways. This captured water can easily double the moisture your plants would otherwise get.

Many landscape architects and designers in southwestern deserts are using something called the "envelope" approach. With this system, your house and the planting areas directly adjacent to the front door and in the courtyard get irrigated in a conventional manner. Here you can keep the indigenous desert plants looking fresher all year, and you can experiment with flowers from other desert regions. You can even keep a few beloved water-guzzlers alive. But outside the envelope, you allow Mother Nature to tend your landscape. There is the true natural desert with all its beauty for you to just sit back and enjoy.

What's wrong with *this* picture? Not a thing!

40

~

Mother Nature's Winter Garden

~

Sally

Most parts of North America look naturally lovely in the winter. Evergreens and snow up north. Evergreens and ever-silvers with golden grasses in the Southwest. Evergreens and ever more evergreens in the Deep South.

And then, there's north central Texas.

This area used to be the Blackland Prairie, the southern tip of the Tallgrass Prairie Biome. Central Oklahoma is in the same boat. Winter is bleak—brown to gray crumpled grasses, bare trees, and a few young eastern red cedars (*Juniperus virginiana*) and a lot of invasive Japanese evergreens.

I found it hard to believe that this one spot on earth had not benefited from Mother Nature's good taste. So one November, while Andy and I were driving down to Houston to visit with friends over the Thanksgiving weekend, I decided to figure out what the Blackland Prairie had really looked like in the winter.

Now, when I'm on the road, I'm a passenger—never a driver if I can help it. Interstate driving is as stimulating as a warm-oil massage; I'm always afraid I'll just nod off. But, as a passenger, I'm free to plant-watch, which is one of my favorite pastimes. By now, I've been down Interstate 45 so many times that I sometimes think I should have every tree and shrub along the way memorized. "Hmm, that boxelder is looking a little peaked this fall. . . ."

On this particular trip, my self-imposed task was to mentally design a winter garden, using only native plants. What I noticed immediately was the lovely winter colors of the native grasses. They were not the taupes and lifeless grays of the nonnative farm and lawn grasses visible in Dallas. There was a soft-looking, short grass that resembled a carpet of the palest yellow fluff. (Picture the color of unsalted butter.) It was beautifully highlighted by sweeps of a taller grass colored a scrumptious russet-orange. (Imagine the heart of a baked sweet potato.) Yummy combination.

Andy, resigned to this sort of thing, pulled off the interstate and let me inspect the grasses. The pale yellow was buffalograss (*Buchloe dactyloides*). The rich orange grass was little bluestem (*Schizachyrium scoparium*). When backlit, it glistened with white tufts of fluffy seed up and down the stems. Nearby in a low place, there was a stand of brushy bluestem (*Andropogon glomeratus*), with thick bushy silvery heads, its stems and leaves coppery and glowing. Both bluestems achieve this beautiful sweet-potato color and remain vibrant throughout the winter until March or April. Good candidates for the winter garden.

Further down the road there were other tall grasses that were a nice tawny gold—Indian grass (*Sorghastrum nutans*). Mentally I placed them next to pale yellow and orange—great idea. When you have such a warm palette of colors, they seem most lively when backed by a cool color. I looked around for a cool color. I didn't have to look far. The clear Virgin Mary–blue sky worked great as a backdrop. But even more inviting were the eastern red cedars (*Juniperus virginiana*). As I glimpsed an occasional yaupon holly (*Ilex vomitoria*) or live oak (*Quercus virginiana*), I was surprised to notice how much more depth and sparkle a juniper added to the scene. Junipers had the richest, most alive green—an eager, thrusting texture that was dark with blue shadows and highlighted with gold. By comparison, the yaupons and oaks had a silvery flatness.

As I composed my winter garden, I wondered how an accent of red-berried possumhaw (*Ilex decidua*) would look in my gold and green color scheme. Obligingly, one leaned over a fence toward me. It looked great. So did a mother yaupon, with translucent red berries peeking out between the leaves.

Then, I tried to picture a purple-berried American beautyberry (*Callicarpa americana*) in my imaginary winter garden. I never saw one, but I did find a knee-high thicket of coralberry (*Symphoricarpus orbicula-tus*). If you think of coral as an orange-red color, you need to re-picture this. Whoever named coralberry was thinking of raspberry-colored coral instead. The purple tones were as satisfying as the red, and my color scheme seemed complete.

I noticed then how the red and purple tones were repeated with the twigs of thicket plum (*Prunus gracilis*). The willows echoed the orange of the bluestems. The papery hanging ornaments of boxelder, and the dark red cornucopias of sumac added even more interest.

On the way home two days later, the sky was leaden and wooly white with a steady drizzle. Yet the plant colors gleamed just as warmly in this dismal light. Mother Nature definitely had aesthetics in mind, as well as more practical matters, when she planned *her* winter garden.

~

Looking for a Good Neighbor? Try a Creek

~

Sally

With the possible exception of W. C. Fields, humans seem to have a natural affinity for water. Maybe it's because we spent the first nine months of our lives immersed in it. Maybe it's because we evolved from sea creatures umpteen million years ago, and the call to return home is programmed into our genes. Or, maybe it's because we're 90 percent water ourselves. Whatever the reason, we gladly pay premium prices for lakefront or oceanside property when an identical home on the same-sized lot a hundred feet inland could be bought for much less.

And, while they avoid water in bathtubs, kids gravitate toward it in creeks and streams; they know that that's where the action is. There are crawfish to hunt and dragonflies to chase and, of course, great walls and dams to be erected from whatever rocks may be found nearby.

Being near water seems to be essential for the good life. And the sound of a creek? Burbling, rushing, singing, trilling—it always seems to fit my mood, whether I want it to be cheerful and stimulating or low-key and restful.

Some of you lucky people live by a creek. If you do, you are also aware that living on a creek—especially a creek in a populated urban area—has a few drawbacks. This is not a perfect world, friends.

Probably the biggest disadvantage is trash. After each rain, it seems as if the contents of every garbage bag in town has washed up on the banks of your creek. I wish I could offer a solution, but I couldn't even get my daughter to keep her room clean. I certainly don't have any ideas about converting our fellow citizens to less messy lives. The only thing to do is budget time and/or money to get the trash cleaned up.

Erosion is another problem. Creeks will just naturally erode; that's how the Grand Canyon happened. But, we're not talking about millions of years here, we're discussing the visible erosion that seems to occur overnight. It happens, generally, as a result of misguided efforts at water control. Some years ago, engineers noticed that parking lots and lawns were contributing a lot of runoff to normal creek flows, and this extra flow was causing flooding. They decided that they would have to get that water moving faster, and the fastest way to move a lot of water, they determined, was to clear the creeks of trees and tall grasses that tend to slow the water down. Some of you may have just bought (or built) a house on a creek that was denuded of vegetation; it's not a pretty sight.

The "experts" are now waking up to the fact that this causes the creeks to erode *too* quickly. Moreover, the soil washed out of them starts building up downstream in lakes and rivers, resulting in more frequent—and costly—dredging operations. We now know that it's more important to *slow* the water down so it has a chance to soak in and help replenish our groundwater supply.

Another problem: Creeks often run dry in the summer. This is nothing new; normally this is caused by droughts and low snowmelt. What *is* new, and a bad sign of the times, is that spring-fed creeks are running dry because the springs themselves are drying up. This occurs because the groundwater that feeds them is not being replenished. Parking lots, streets, and compacted lawns do not allow rain to soak into the ground. Sometimes the local water board even lets someone buy all of your groundwater for watering a golf course or running a factory.

Still another difficulty concerns ownership. With creeks, you often own only to the middle of the creek bed, and someone else owns the other half. As a result, your view of the creek includes the opposite bank, over which you have no control. If your neighbor is a talented and tasteful gardener, count yourself lucky. Your neighbor might be a connoisseur of junked autos, proudly displaying his collection of rusty and mangled auto carcasses right across from your sundeck.

Even with all of these problems, a creek is a wonderful thing to have on your land. It offers you the possibility of having a little bit of Eden in your own backyard. You can hear gurgling water at least part of the year, and you can hear birds chirping all year long. And, you can make all of these surroundings as wild or as tame as you choose.

Of course, it's actually the vegetation found along a creek that makes it pretty and attractive to wildlife. The trees and groundcovers that have grown up the banks and out of the water are the typical woodland plants for the area and will vary considerably from one part of the country to the next. The trees right along the banks, within one or two feet of the water, are almost universal: sycamores, cottonwoods, boxelder, and willows are the most common, with bald cypress or river birch often found in swampy areas in the South and alders in the North.

Because life along a creek is only safe until the next flood, creek plants are different from other plants. They have aggressive, wide-ranging roots for holding tight to the bank and the bit of soil they occupy. The smaller plants sucker extensively, and any bit of root that is washed away is capable of making a new plant wherever it ends up downstream. The trees grow fast and die young. The trick is getting established quickly and being able to reestablish quickly. Longevity and high quality are not rewarded.

If your stream is denuded of trees and you want to change this, look around. You'll probably find numerous seedlings. If you're lucky, you'll have a large amount of saplings or adolescent seedlings. You won't need all of them, but quite a few might be useful. Mark them with flagging tape so you won't accidentally destroy them. Choose the ones that are tallest or best placed for your landscape scheme, and pull up the rest. Let some stay clumped together and leave plenty along the fastest eroding part of your creek to help hold the bank. These will become your canopy of shade trees.

Before you pull up any seedlings, add stakes (or lawn chairs or whatever) by the young trees you want to keep. Imagine how these young trees will look when they're all grown up. Look at them from all of the most important windows in your house, as well as from any outside seating areas. If it is too hard to picture, have your friends stand beside them and pretend to be trees. (Is this a theme party idea?) You'll probably change your mind quite a few times before you're satisfied with your arrangement of seedlings.

If you're impatient to gain some height in your landscape, you can buy a few native bottomland trees to give you comfort for the first year. If you have more patience than money, don't worry; your landscape will grow much faster than you'd imagine, probably as fast as one containing purchased trees. Plus, by using what has established there naturally, you will have exactly the trees with the right genetic makeup for your creek.

Once you have an idea of where most of your trees will be located, plan your overall scheme. Can you dam to create a little pool of slower-moving water that can be maintained at a dependable height? (You'll need permission from the county to do this.) Can you get lots of sun to this spot for hibiscus and other water plants that require plenty of light? Or, will a totally wooded setting fit in best with your neighbors' landscapes? Do you need evergreen screening for one part, or do you have enough room for a more natural looking thicket of deciduous trees mixed with evergreens? Planning is easiest if you can draw your ideas on paper. See if you can find your land survey. This is often called a plat plan and is usually one of the pieces of paper you get (and pay for) when you buy your house. It shows your property lines, utility easements, the hundred-year flood line, and the exact position of your house on your property. Sometimes, it also shows the location of a few especially large trees. Check the scale. Most often, it is twenty feet to the inch but is sometimes sixty feet to the inch or some other number. Measure a few key boundaries to make sure your survey was done accurately. Then, have a couple of copies made.

Now, you're ready to draw. Block out where you want woods, where you want seating areas, paths, stairs, and so on. Plot your existing trees, both young and old.

Once you have the walking areas and the shade trees in place, you get to the really fun part. Now you can plan the flowering trees and ground-covers that will make your creek area a special garden. Plant lots of understory trees with low shrubs or woodland flowers and ferns for groundcover. Plant thickets or evergreens for screening. Remember, the actual plants you choose need to be appropriate for the creeks where you live. Here are some samples of what you might do:

In tallgrass prairie areas along a sunny creek, plant indigo bush (*Amorpha fruticosa*). If the water level is more dependable because of a dam, and you have plenty of sun, you could also plant buttonbush (*Cephalanthus occidentalis*). Both are bushes that can eventually become very large shrubs or small trees. The amorpha has purple spikes in the spring. The buttonbush has fragrant white globes of flowers all summer that attract butterflies.

At the feet of these shrubs you could plant a groundcover of frogfruit (*Phyla* spp.), with asters, goldenrods, and sunflowers. For a rich winter color of cinnamon orange, plant a clump of brushy bluestem (*Andropogon glomeratus*), if it grows in your area. If not, try switchgrass (*Panicum virgatum*), with its feathery plumes and dark golden fall color. All of these plants like at least a half a day of sun and are excellent for erosion control.

In the Southeast, creeks tend to be deeply shaded. Plant blooming understory trees on the banks with blue-flowered ruellia, amsonia, or phlox beneath. At the muddy edge, have a groundcover of white-blooming lizard's tails (*Saururus cernuus*) with chain fern (*Woodwardia areolata*) just barely up the bank beneath a thicket of Virginia sweetspire (*Itea virginica*). In a sunny spot, plant inland seaoats (*Chasmanthium latifolium*) with their gorgeous dangling seed heads. Screen with evergreen yaupon holly (*Ilex vomitoria*) or a thicket of strawberrybush (*Euonymus americana*).

Further north, use a thicket of red-stemmed dogwood (*Cornus sericea*) or red-berried common winterberry (*Ilex verticillata*). For evergreens, use inkberry holly (*Ilex glabra*), American holly (*Ilex opaca*), or bayberry (*Myrica pensylvanica*).

Along the Gulf Coast, screen with wax myrtle (*Myrica cerifera*) and plant palmettos (*Sabal minor*) and scarlet sage (*Salvia coccinea*) under swamp haw (*Viburnum nudum*).

In the Southwest, you're definitely into arroyo, not creek, country. Desert willow (*Chilopsis linearis*) and other trees requiring good drainage—but grateful for the underground water and the shade cast by the arroyo banksides—grow along the arroyos with showy Apache plume (*Fallugia paradoxia*) and numerous wildflowers. These plants are often protected by river stones that prevent floodwater from unearthing them.

In the Northwest, plant Rocky Mountain maple (*Acer glabrum*) and the gorgeous orange-fruited mountain ash (*Sorbus scopulina*) under larger trees with twinberry (*Lonicera involucrata*) and numerous woodlands sedges and flowers, like the dramatic goatbeard (*Aruncus dioicus* var. *acuminatus*). In sun, stream banks are often lined with thickets of wild rose (*Rosa woodsii*), Saskatoon serviceberry (*Amelanchier alnifolia*), and red osier (*Cornus sericea*). I also recommend the fragrant white-flowered Lewis's mockorange (*Philadelphus lewisii*) and the weedy but colorful red elderberry (*Sambucus racemosa*).

For those of you with fully planted creeks where it would take a machete to get through to the water, your job is not planting, it's pruning. At first, cut out the invasive plants such as trash trees and Japanese honeysuckle. If you still can't reach the water, cut a narrow path by removing saplings of the dominant shade trees.

Observe your woods for a full year. Each time something blooms or fruits or otherwise proves itself worthy, tie a ribbon around it. The ribbon means that plant is sacrosanct; everything else is a candidate for thinning out—unless, of course, you've grown to love the surprises and treats that Mother Nature provides in a dense woods. If so, just let her have her way while you sit back and enjoy.

PART VII

Where Do We Go from Here?

The sun, the moon, and the stars would have
disappeared long ago, had they happened to
be within reach of predatory human hands.

—HAVELOCK ELLIS

I would argue that just the turning of our attention
to the natural world tends to subvert our anthro-
pocentric heritage. We may be on some sort of a
halting journey toward understanding the world,
and ourselves within it, as one system.

—THOMAS J. LYON,
This Incomperable Lande

~

The Eighth Deadly Sin

~

Sally and Andy

One of the reasons we love Albee, our CPA, is that he works wonders when it comes to finding us every possible—and legitimate—tax break. Nothing wrong with that. But sometimes legitimate tax breaks can cause environmental problems. For example, we recall visiting a friend's Texas Hill Country ranch some years back and enjoying the spectacular view from her kitchen window. But what we next saw out that window was a rape in progress.

One of her neighbors became aware of the hefty tax breaks the state gives to ranchers for clearing their land and turning it into pasture. The bitter irony is that this land will never become pasture; the hills are too steep to grow grass, and the soil is too thin. What *does* grow there very well is Ashe juniper, twistleaf yucca, prickly pear cactus, and an assortment of wildflowers—all of which this guy had bulldozed away, leaving a scarred and erosion-prone landscape.

In most states, tax laws do not encourage land conservation. Landowners are penalized for allowing land to lie fallow and regenerate itself. A rancher and his or her survivors can never retire; the ranch must be worked to qualify for tax breaks. If they just want to sit on their backsides and sip cool drinks in their golden years, they're going to have to pay much higher, very likely unaffordable, taxes for the privilege. Either that or sell off the land that has probably been in their family for generations and move away to a condo.

Of course, ranching, even with subsidies, is no quick and easy path to riches. We're all eating less red meat these days—not just because we're more cholesterol-conscious, but because we are learning more about the way cattle are raised. Steak houses brag about their "corn-fed beef." Now we know that cattle don't digest corn well at all and frequently develop gastrointestinal problems requiring massive doses of antibiotics, which then show up in the T-bones and ribeyes we eat, and ultimately in our bodies. Everybody knows that antibiotics wipe out our bodies' natural immune systems, leaving us more vulnerable to infections than we would be otherwise.

Many ranches are being sold to wealthy urbanites who want to escape the frenetic city life and enjoy the beauty of the wide open spaces. These city slickers don't want to actually *be* ranchers, but when faced with the choice of paying higher taxes or running a few head of cattle on their spread, they quickly opt for the cows.

Our friend's neighbor got his tax breaks. But at what a cost. Those once-lovely hills now look like a devastated wasteland, and will for generations to come. Possibly forever. This land, like the desert, heals very, very slowly. With no roots to hold it, the topsoil washes away and so does its store of native seeds. That hill, instead of being green, may become a bare limestone knob.

Sally's own parents benefited from similar tax laws. Back in the mid-sixties, they purchased 180 acres of forest and meadow in East Texas. They were told that if they planted commercial pine trees in the meadow, they'd get substantial tax savings. So, they did. And a once healthy and thriving forty-acre meadow habitat was turned into an environmentally sterile tree farm with hundreds of slash pines lined up like cadets. Back in those days, few of us were thinking about conservation. Besides, it would take a saint to say, "Thanks, but forget those tax savings. I'll just preserve the landscape and pay through the nose for the privilege." The point is that too many states have antiquated tax laws that encourage the degradation of the land, and discourage conservation.

And you thought you had to go to the Brazilian rain forests to see how we mistreat Mother Nature!

There's another ranch out in Bosque County, west of Waco, that Sally got to visit in her professional capacity as a landscape designer. The owners hired her to come out, look around, tell them what was growing there, how they could preserve what needed preserving, get rid of what needed getting rid of, and draw up a landscape plan for around the main house. It was a treat because she didn't see one single non-native plant on the entire spread.

So what? So this: It's very rare these days to see countryside that *is* all native. Weeds from Europe, Asia, and Africa are so widespread and prevalent that most people are amazed to learn that they don't actually belong there, that they are invaders.

As Sally explored the Bosque County ranch, she didn't see a single Japanese honeysuckle smothering the live oaks and viburnums. There was no Johnson grass, Bermuda grass, or African bluestem grasses crowding out the feathery, delicately colored, gently waving meadow of native grama grasses with its sprinkling of little bluestem and flowers.

Yet, as beautiful as this rugged ranchland is, it has been shaped domestic grazing. Agronomists (grass experts) claim that the current palette of grasses is very different from what the first settlers saw.

More than a century and a half ago, before this land was subjected to European grazing practices, there would have been a prairie dominated by little bluestem, big bluestem, and Indian grass. Only in the poorer soils that couldn't hold plenty of water and organic matter would there have been gramas and other short grasses. There would have been no patches of bare earth showing between the clumps of grass.

Farm and ranch lands all over America are sadly depleted—ruined by European farming practices that are better suited to deeper soils and higher rainfalls. Pastures are fenced in, changing the feeding habits of cattle. Once, when cows grazed on open rangeland, they nibbled on their favorite bits of vegetation, then moved on in search of more. Fenced in, they are forced to eat what is available—and *only* what is there. The land is soon overgrazed to the point of desolation.

Overgrazing is not the only culprit. Long ago, plowing destroyed the prairie sod, allowing wind and rainstorms to erode the topsoils off of the fields. Rainwater now runs off; it doesn't soak into aquifers, natural underground water storage areas that keep springs and creeks running when no rain has fallen for months. The entire natural cycle of the land and all of the life it supports is disturbed.

Clearly, it isn't only outdated land-use laws that contribute to the degradation of the land. Our point of view is also flawed. We look at land as something to be consumed and exploited, not as a resource to be cherished for the long haul.

Some years back, while we were still living in Big D, the music station Andy was tuned into followed Mendelssohn's *Italian Symphony* with a one-minute inspirational message from a local church. The message really hit home, and he couldn't help but think of those ranches.

The message was called "Species Pride," and it was delivered by the Reverend Hal Brady, former pastor of Dallas's First United Methodist Church. Brady reminded us that "of all our sins and shortcomings . . . species pride is the one most frequently ignored. The sin of species pride is when we humans become arrogant in our human-centeredness. In relation to plants, animals, the earth, the environment, and the rest of creation, we place an overemphasis on *dominion* and an underemphasis on the *interdependence of all created life*."

Of course, it's not difficult to see how we got this way. First, we had biblical sanction. We were told clearly in Genesis that we were put here "to replenish the earth and subdue it." We're doing great on the subdue part, anyway.

Our forebears didn't see anything wrong with subduing and exploiting the earth. After all, there was plenty of everything around for everybody, and it was unimaginable to them that the vast forests might in fact be finite, that the mighty oceans might get gunked up with garbage and industrial waste. Brady concluded by saying, "Today, of course, we know better." Well, maybe. Some of us do, but too many members of our species still haven't got a clue. We elect a lot of them.

Our plan to save our vanishing wildlands must start by having state legislatures recognize conservation as a valid land use, allowing landowners the same tax breaks for maintaining natural habitats that they receive for farming or ranching. In 1991, Texas took an encouraging step in that direction by passing a law that recognizes "wildlife management" as an "agricultural use." This is primarily to benefit those farmers and ranchers who lease out hunting rights, but many of our native habitats will benefit.

And in North Carolina, their revised land-use tax laws are widely regarded as environmental models for other states to follow. Similar legislation is currently pending in other states, including Delaware, Colorado, Hawaii, and Wisconsin.

Land conservation is not just a problem for rural communities. The preservation of our land, water, and wildlife is vital to all of us. It is impor-

tant that we all learn about land management, and let our state representatives know how we feel.

Remember the story of Noah's Ark? Noah was charged with collecting
and saving two of every animal species—we assume God meant a male and
female—so that they could survive the Great Flood. Modern genetics
tells us that just two won't cut it. Today, many species numbering in the
hundreds lack sufficient genetic diversity to survive and are in danger of
extinction. Beyond that, some species need a minimum of 200,000 contiguous acres to survive, and that much space isn't available—not unless
landowners and municipalities jointly make the decision to provide it. This
earth is our ark. Our charge is Noah's. Our instructions are clear.

"Car 88, proceed to 143 Edison Street. Couple growing penstemons and coneflowers in front yard!"

43

∽

Weeding Out
Bad Weed Laws

∽

Andy

June 3, 1994, was an ideal day for a home garden tour in Tulsa, Oklahoma—the weather was balmy and the plants were in full bloom. Over 800 people visited Evelyn Connor's garden that day, one of eight on the itinerary, and they had been very impressed by her lush naturalistic (natives and nonnatives) landscape that included mullein pinks, a variety of poppies, and a mass of three-foot-high native purple coneflowers.

The mailman also came to Evelyn's home that day, but not to appreciate the flowers; he delivered a citation from the city charging the eighty-two-year-old widow with violating Tulsa's weed ordinances. City officials never actually saw Evelyn's garden; they simply reacted to an anonymous neighbor who had phoned in a complaint about Evelyn's front yard, calling her wildflowers "weeds," and demanding that they be mowed down.

Evelyn started making a few phone calls of her own. The first was to a friend and fellow gardener at *The Tulsa World*, and by the next day her plight made the front page, not just locally, but all over the country. The

Associated Press picked up her story, TV stations sent out crews to inter-
view her, and she received a flood of encouraging letters from well-wishers,
including school children who mailed her drawings of wildflowers. Calls
and letters also started arriving at City Hall. It didn't take long for the city
of Tulsa to figure out that it had picked on the wrong eighty-two-year-old
widow! The city apologized, withdrew the complaint, and changed the
ordinance so as to be more protective of naturalistic landscapes.

While this story is charming and inspiring (at one time, a made-for-TV
movie had been planned), here's one that is downright bizarre.

Up in Toronto, Canada, Douglas Counter ran up against the same
municipal attitude that Evelyn found in Tulsa. Ironically, in 1998, his
"offending" garden had been on a city-sponsored garden tour designed to
promote naturalistic landscaping. That same year, Mayor Mel Lastman presented Doug with an award recognizing his environmental commitment.
And in 1999 and again in 2001, Doug's garden was nominated for the City
of Toronto Garden Award. Now he's in court, and the decision will be
precedent setting.

The natural landscape of Walter and Nancy Stewart of Potomac,
Maryland, was once called "disgraceful" by an anonymous neighbor who
stuck a warning note in their mailbox. Cited by the city, they prepared for
their day in court. "When the city saw our witness list—people from The
Aububon Society and other leading environmentalists," Walter recalls, "and
when our story got told on *Good Morning America*, the city backed off.
Not only that, but they revised the ordinance to allow for a set-back."
Today, Walter reports that a number of their neighbors now are trying natural areas on their own properties.

More sobering is the story of Myrdene Anderson, of West Lafayette,
Indiana. A professor of anthropology at Purdue University, Myrdene is also
a natural gardener. Her neighbors are not, and were infuriated by her
"prairie thicket" of prairie grass, native trees, and wildflowers. They filed a
petition asking the city to make her mow it all down to what they considered an acceptable height. The city then cited her, and Myrdene found her-
self looking at a penalty of $500 for every day she refused to mow. Did she
buckle? No way. She dug in her heels, hired a lawyer (eventually two), and
fought the citation.

Myrdene, like Evelyn Connor, got a lot of positive publicity in the local
press and moral support from friends and strangers alike. And when she
threatened to take the case to court, the city had second thoughts and a
settlement was reached. Myrdene's landscape had to be inspected twice
a year for five years by a retired forester that both sides agreed on—and *she*

had to foot the bill for the inspection at $100 per visit! That, plus legal fees, wound up costing Myrdene "many thousands of dollars"—just so she could landscape in an environmentally correct way. Some of her neighbors are still not happy, but Myrdene believes the fight was well worth fighting— and says she'd do it all again.

The sad fact is that in many communities, in both the United States and Canada, homeowners who choose to deviate from the conventional landscape look—well-trimmed lawns and clipped boxhedges—run the risk of being cited and fined. (By the way, outrageous weed laws are not limited to North America; Reuters reported on April 9, 2002, that Gloria Cisternas, a housewife in Providencia, Chile, was sentenced to seven days in jail for refusing to keep a grassy patch in front of her home.)

Going to court is an extreme step that most people would rather avoid, says Bret Rappaport, a Chicago attorney who specializes in fighting weed laws. Instead, he believes that educating people about the benefits of natural landscapes will go a long way toward ending discriminatory weed laws. He likes to quote conservationist Baba Dioum who wrote, "We will conserve only what we love, we will love only what we understand, and we will understand only what we are taught."

In most cases, Rappaport asserts, traditional weed ordinances are used against natural landscapers, not out of vindictiveness or meanness, but out of ignorance. "It's not really surprising," he says. "We all grew up with the conventional lawn landscape. It never occurs to most people to try anything else . . . in spite of the fact that mowing and edging and bagging are not among our favorite pastimes. And nobody likes the noise pollution generated by power mowers and blowers."

People tend to label as weeds any plants they aren't familiar with and which aren't standard nursery stock. Native plants are often mistakenly called "weeds." In fact, weeds do not occur in nature. Weeds are alien invaders that thrive in disturbed areas. Common bermudagrass, nutgrass, and crabgrass are just a few of the more common ones. Often they arrive in home landscapes with a truckload of topsoil.

Another common misconception is the fear that natural landscapes harbor rats and vermin. In fact, these creatures live in garbage, not in well-maintained natural landscapes.

Rappaport makes it clear that he is not against the concept of weed ordinances. "Some people," he says, "just don't care how their yards look. They let things get out of hand and their yards look trashy and hurt the neighborhood. Weed ordinances help control that sort of run-amok landscape."

What he *is* against, he states, is when these ordinances are used as weapons against neighbors who do not conform to the standard, "acceptable" look. "We grant our neighbors the right to have shaved lawns or colored gravel, tacky concrete statuary, plastic sunflowers, and Astroturf on the front porch," says Rappaport. "It's only fair that we also grant homeowners the right to have natural landscapes, which are far more beneficial. They reduce watering, eliminate the need for chemical pesticides, and provide sanctuaries for songbirds, butterflies, and a host of other desirable wildlife. They also need a lot less maintenance."

Instead of overthrowing weed laws, he says, they should be rewritten so that they take into account both the community's aesthetic concerns and an individual's right of self-expression.

One approach that is being adopted by communities across the country is the "set-back" ordinance. "Imagine a wall with a splash of paint on it," says Rappaport. "You'd say it was a mess. But put a picture frame around that splash and you might say it was modern art. It might not be *your* idea of great art, but you could accept it as something more than just a messy paint splotch."

"Now imagine a natural landscape: wildflowers, groundcovers, shrubs, accent grasses, trees—the whole nine yards—all growing much as they do in nature. Some people find this offensive as a neighborhood landscape. But what if the homeowner had a two- to five-foot low border around this natural area . . . maybe grass, maybe a low growing groundcover. Now it has a landscaped, *planned* look. Again, it might not be a neighbor's idea of a traditional landscape look, but it has become more acceptable."

Bret Rappaport suggests that neighbors can also be pacified by adding an obvious human touch here and there: a stone walkway, a bench, a water feature . . . something that says: this landscape was planned, it didn't just happen. "It's amazing what a difference this can make in community attitudes."

Largely because of his involvement with weed laws, Rappaport has become an advocate of natural landscaping. "We have to understand," he says, "that we do not live *apart* from nature, we *are* a part of nature."

For more information about combating unfair weed ordinances, write to The John Marshall Law School for a copy of Bret Rappaport's article in the summer 1993 issue of *The John Marshall Law Review*, vol. 26, no. 4. The address is 315 South Plymouth Court, Chicago, IL 60604. Include a check or money order for $5 plus postage.

44

◈

Where Have All the Saplings Gone, Long Time Passing?

◈

Sally

White Rock Lake is a very pleasant body of water in our old Dallas neighborhood. It is home to waterfowl, fish, at least one beaver, and—on the first warm weekend of spring—an army of riffraff and lowlifes who play their car radios at eardrum-breaking levels and then depart, leaving the lake ringed with empty beer cans, fried chicken boxes, and Styrofoam cups.

The lake used to be far from the outskirts of town; it didn't move, Dallas did. Today, White Rock Lake is considered practically downtown. When it was dammed in the 1920s to become the water reservoir for the City, the surrounding land became a park. For the last eighty years, its banks have been mowed by the Parks Department—except for where it's been so well trod by fishermen and picnickers that there's nothing left to mow.

During those eighty years, the willows and cottonwoods have become huge and geriatric. The shorter-lived understory trees have died. As you stroll around the lakeshore, you can't help but notice that there are no seedlings, no saplings, and no young trees at all. For eighty years, no young trees have been allowed to replace the aging giants. Now the city must embark on a very expensive planting program. If areas had been mowed around and left natural, this would not have been necessary. Trees would have had a chance to regenerate.

In the Hill Country of central Texas, there are any number of farms and ranches where you can't find a tree that is younger than one hundred years old. Huge lindens, cherries, live oaks, and post oaks dominate the scene. The only smaller trees I've seen in my survey of several ranches are Bigelow oak (called scrub oak) and rusty blackhaw viburnum (*V. rufidulum*). These trees are all exceptionally long-lived.

Why aren't there any babies to carry on the line? Why aren't there redbuds, sumacs, Hercules clubs, or any other small trees so prevalent along the roadsides? For over one hundred years, something's been happening to all of the seedling trees.

In the Hill Country, they were gobbled up. In the early part of this century, farmers overstocked with sheep and goats; another drought followed. Both the land and the farmers have been trying to recover since then.

In an effort to save the livestock, ranchers declared open season on wolves, coyotes, and mountain lions. At the same time, the screwworm and other livestock parasites were brought under control. All of this fostered a proliferation of deer. The deer in the Hill Country are half the size they used to be—too many deer for too little vegetation. The cattle eat the grasses and flowers. The deer browse the deciduous trees and shrubs. And what is left? Juniper-covered hillsides.

I am especially concerned when I see post oak lands, where grazing or mowing prevented regeneration for over a century and now housing developments are moving in. Post oaks (*Quercus stellata*) are the principal canopy tree for an enormous portion of the United States. Traditionally, they grew in dry woodlands and savannas between the lush eastern forests and the tallgrass prairies. When I hear doggerel about "mighty oaks," I immediately picture post oaks. These are big spreading trees with strong, gnarled limbs; there are no wimpy twigs. Periodic fires kept them spaced far apart, allowing them to develop broad, spreading limbs. They form thick, corky bark to withstand these fires. They look burly and tough. But that macho look is deceptive. They're very sensitive to bulldozers, cement, and chemicals (like all other trees), but they're also sensitive to irrigation. Yes, irrigation. The way it's been explained to me, post oak roots are stiff and stubby, and the hair roots that do the actual work are accustomed to large amounts of oxygen in the soil. When the soil is compacted by construction and then overwatered by homeowners who put in thirsty plants that are mismatched with the original environment, the post oaks literally suffocate.

This scenario is also true for black oaks (*Quercus velutina*) and their numerous hybrids. Native to the eastern half of the United States, these majestic oaks, like the more southerly post oaks, were on the sandy soils farmers usually didn't bother to plow. And so they survived, while the richer-soiled savannas composed of bur oaks and white oaks have long been extinct. Now, they are immensely popular for new suburbs where a tree over ten feet tall is a real treat. But sprinkler systems can undo all the work of saving the big old trees, and lawnmowers, like cattle, will destroy new seedlings.

Look around your neighborhood, wherever you live. If the trees are getting old and there are no youngsters to replace them, take action. One obvious and easy way to help tree seedlings get established is temporary fencing. Fencing keeps mowers or livestock from destroying all of the seedlings, allowing some to grow into saplings. When the saplings get old enough to be less vulnerable, remove the fencing and thin them out so they will not become overcrowded.

There are other solutions, too. For individual trees, you can install tree tubes around very young saplings to protect them from mowers and other urban hazards, such as rambunctious little boys.

Less unsightly methods can be used. If you do your own maintenance, you can establish a mow line, a graceful curving line of natural area bordered by a mowed path or lawn. Don't worry at first about planting this area. Just observe whatever comes up. Short-lived weeds like dandelions and clover will disappear as shade develops. Eradicate only the noxious weeds such as garlic mustard (*Alliaria petiolata*) or European buckthorn (*Rhamnus cathartica*). If you want to set aside a permanent wooded area, you can delineate and protect the prospective natural woodland with an attractive wall of stone.

There is a twofold advantage in allowing your native trees to seed out. First, the costs are dramatically lower than buying, planting, and watering nursery-grown trees. Second, instead of planting ill-adapted or environmentally harmful trees, you are preserving the very trees and gene pools that are tailor-made by Mother Nature for where you live.

~

The Fad That Won't Go Away!

~

Andy

While giving a speech at the Dallas Arboretum in 1993, Peter Olin, director of the Minnesota Landscape Arboretum, dismissed the naturalistic landscaping movement as a "craze." In other words, a fad!

Well, according to my dictionary, a fad is "a temporary fashion." It is described as "a pursuit or interest followed, usually widely but briefly and capriciously, with exaggerated zeal." Fads are skinny trousers one year and bell-bottoms the next. Fads are hula hoops, mood rings, zoot suits, Nehru jackets, Tiny Tim, purple cars, Beanie Babies, and (one can only hope) blue nail polish.

No way can anyone add native/naturalistic landscaping to that list. Interest and enthusiasm for natural landscaping have been growing slowly but steadily . . . gaining in popularity year by year, yet not overwhelming us in a paroxysm of ardor that would threaten to trivialize its very real value. As author Ken Druse says in his book, *The Natural Habitat*, "What we found was that a grassroots movement (of natural landscapes) was quietly sweeping across the United States, one garden at a time."

The native/naturalistic landscaping trend really got going in the early 1980s. And if anyone doubts that this is a movement with "legs" and a bright future, look at what's happened to it since:

- National gardening publications (*Fine Gardening, The American Gardener*, etc.) that rarely if ever mentioned natives in the past, now routinely include features on native gardening in every issue. This is also true for gardening programs on radio and television.
- Where once it was difficult if not impossible to find books on native plants, today there is a growing library of successful books by authors such as Sara Stein, Ken Druse, Janet Marinelli, Leslie Sauer, Jim Wilson, Lorraine Johnson, Carol Ottesen, and others.
- In 1994, President Clinton issued a presidential directive stating that all federal buildings and installations should landscape with plants native to their areas. This directive has met with widespread acceptance. And to date it has not been rescinded by the current administration.
- Virtually every state has a native plant society, and they are adding members and chapters all the time. *The Wild Ones*, an organization devoted to natural landscaping, is the closest thing we have to a national native plant society; they currently have chapters in eleven states.
- Master Gardeners and other garden clubs are now embracing naturalistic and environmental gardening.
- Significantly, nurseries that specialize in native plants (i.e., 50 percent or more of their stock is devoted to natives) have gone from a mere handful fifteen years ago to many hundreds. As one native nursery owner told me, "I can only sell what people will buy. This business is too hard for me to be a pioneer promoting plants that people don't want." In Texas, there are now close to one hundred native nurseries, and in Florida, native plants have become a $101 million-per-year industry.
- Native demonstration gardens are now an important and popular part of most botanic gardens around the country: Cheekwood Gardens in Nashville, Calloway Gardens in Georgia, Morton Arboretum in Chicago, and Strybing Arboretum in San Francisco to name a few. Perhaps this was inspired in part by exclusively native gardens that have been around awhile, such as Rancho Santa Ana in Claremont, California, Santa Barbara Botanic Garden in Santa Barbara, California, and Garden in the Woods in Massachusetts.

- Water departments all over the country are promoting *xeriscaping*, a technique for water-smart landscaping that makes native plants an important part of the program. Xeriscape homes have shown significantly less water consumption—from 30 to 60 percent.
- Major corporations are trading vast expanses of high-maintenance and water-guzzling lawns for native/naturalistic landscaping. Sears national headquarters outside Chicago, United Parcel Service in Atlanta, and GE Marquette Electronics in Milwaukee are just three of many.

Where will the native/naturalistic landscaping movement be in the next twenty to thirty years? According to Dr. David Northington, former executive director of the Lady Bird Johnson Wildflower Center in Austin, Texas, native landscapes will, by then, have become the norm. "The concept of using regional native wildflowers, grasses, shrubs, vines, and trees in our home and commercial landscapes will," he says, "have turned the corner. It will no longer be thought of as an interesting but esoteric notion appealing only to a select audience." The lawn-centered landscapes of today, he added, will be seen as examples of our wasteful past.

Think this is unlikely? Then consider this scenario: What if back in 1975 you and I were chatting, and I told you that by the end of the twentieth century we'd be living in a society with smoke-free restaurants, smoke-free airline flights, and smoke-free workplaces, and that if you go to a party with fifty guests, only one person will be smoking. Out on the patio. And it'll be a woman. Well, you'd have said I was nuts! And yet look what's happened.

The rise of the native/naturalistic landscape won't happen because of aesthetics, or even because it reduces upkeep. It will happen for one inescapable and pragmatic reason. Continuing water shortages will drive up the cost of this precious resource, making today's conventional landscapes not only impractical but, as Northington points out, "possibly even unpatriotic."

Some people still aren't convinced. May never be. And I must admit, there are days when I get a little pessimistic. I talk to a landscape architect at a conference back east; he tells me how he designed a "fantastic" naturalistic landscape for a bank. One day he drives by and—his landscape is gone, replaced by a carpet of turf grass. He inquires and is told that the bank's biggest depositor saw the native landscape and demanded that "those weeds" be removed and a "decent" landscape put in its place. I hear from another landscape architect whose biggest client demanded that, before any other work was done, all the trees on his property be cut down! And I hear from a designer whose drought-tolerant, regionally correct landscape for a town's visitor center was rejected because the maintenance people would work only with familiar nursery stock, most of which was unsuited to the town's dry climate. Those are the days I become pessimistic.

But then there are days like the one several years ago when I was in Wisconsin doing photography for one of our books. I wanted a photo of a typical lawn maintenance crew, and spotted one as I drove through a suburban neighborhood.

I approached the guy who seemed to be in charge. His name was Gerry Conkle, and he owned the company. I asked him if he and his partner would pose for my camera and, naturally, he asked me why I wanted it. I hesitated. After all, one of the primary themes of the books Sally and I do is low-maintenance. We were, in effect, trying to put Gerry and his colleagues out of business. Fat chance he'd pose for me if he knew that!

But I told him anyway and, to my surprise, he consented. Then he added, "Y'know, I guess I'm part of this environmental gardening movement, too." I looked at his power mowers and leaf blowers, and thought, "Uh huh." But then he said, "Back a few years part of my business was applying lawn chemicals—herbicides and pesticides. But then I got to reading about what these chemicals can do to you, and I decided to eliminate that part of my service. I want to be around to play with my grandkids someday."

A passing fad? Not a chance!

"Mind if I tag along? My habitat got wiped out!"

~

CHAPTER 46

The Big Backlash!

~

Andy

Whenever a new idea or movement shows signs of gaining popularity, there is a backlash of adverse publicity. What happens when a new diet book reaches best-seller status? The critics come out in droves. And remember when rock 'n roll first came on the scene? It was called "an invention of the Devil!"

Did we really think the native plant movement would be an exception?

Over the past decade, I've encountered a number of negative articles on native plants and natural landscaping—ranging from merely misinformed to downright bizarre to clearly hostile.

One writer in a national gardening magazine maintained that it was impossible to be successful with native plants unless one was "willing to live like a bear in the wilderness." Another—a professor of horticulture no less—described natural landscapes as "messy and unkempt." And, more recently, the editor of a publication aimed at the nursery trade devoted its editorial page to telling readers why natives were overrated, and bolstered his argument with over a dozen "facts"—all demonstrably wrong.

Perhaps the two best-known examples came to the public via two of our most prestigious publications. In May 1994, the *New York Times Magazine* ran Michael Pollan's polemic, "Against Nativism," which stated, among other things, that "the natural gardening movement has all but seized control of official taste in this country." When I read this, I had to wonder if he was referring to some country other than the United States. This was akin to saying that General Custer had seized control of the Sioux nation at the Little Big Horn!

That there is a natural gardening movement, and that it is growing in size and stature, I readily admit. But I can only wish that it were as influential as Pollan maintained. A stroll through most nurseries and garden centers, or a drive through virtually any suburban neighborhood, quickly reveals the truth: North America is still in the grip of the traditional lawn-boxhedge-topiary landscape, and one must still search diligently to locate natural or naturalistic landscapes.

Pollan's article seemed to imply that advocates of native/natural landscaping are latter day storm troopers. And to drive this preposterous notion home, he quoted a couple of garden historians who connect Germany's pre–World War II natural gardening movement with "nationalistic and racist ideas."

Every organization, philosophy, and movement attracts a few fringe loonies, but countless people that Sally and I know who are drawn to natural gardening are as tyrannical as Santa Claus. Which is not to say they aren't opinionated and passionate. It's been our experience that when you get ten native plant enthusiasts together, you'll hear at least seven or eight differing opinions on whatever topic you toss at them; that's one reason why hanging around a native plant society meeting can be such fun.

Pollan's fictitious "Nazi" garden "grants citizenship exclusively to native plants," "outlaws any human artifice in its designs," and "bans the 'brutal' practice of pruning."

To refute this, we must first make the distinction between a natural garden and a natural*istic* garden. The natural garden is a preserved habitat, just the way Mother Nature designed it, or a recreated landscape that mimics the old gal's work. Here, only native plants are suitable, and exotic "volunteer" plants that may have appeared over the years are ousted. But this is common sense. To make an authentic Caesar salad, you don't add sliced tomatoes and radishes. For an authentic natural landscape, you don't add hostas and begonias.

A natural*istic* landscape is another matter. A naturalistic landscape or garden resembles Mother Nature's handiwork—to a point. It is not tightly structured and symmetrical, but informal and casual. Plants that are not native to the site, but are still well adapted, can be used.

Pruning is not banned, nor is it labeled as a brutal practice. Judicious pruning is a necessary part of the upkeep of both a naturalistic *and* natural landscape. What *is* discouraged for these types of gardens is the curious "art" of topiary (see chapter 19). And "human artifice," such as water features, meandering walkways, statuary, and lighting, are not "outlawed," but are used frequently and creatively.

Does Pollan find natural and naturalistic landscapes too "subtle"? Personally, I've never thought of New England's native woodlands in the autumn, the Texas Hill Country ablaze with spring wildflowers, or a vista of prairie grasses backlit by the setting sun as yawn-provoking. But apparently some gardeners require bold bursts of vibrant exotic color in crisply designated rows and squared-off beds to be truly satisfying. It just ain't a garden, Pollan seems to be telling us, unless it looks controlled and contrived and meddled with. I'm reminded of something a lady friend once told me about cosmetics: The best makeup job is one that looks like you aren't wearing any . . . as opposed to the Tammy Faye school of cosmetology.

Recently, Sally and I drove along the west coast from northern California to British Columbia. In Victoria, we paid an obligatory visit to the famous Butchart Gardens, expecting to be wowed by its much-praised and ballyhooed botanical displays. But the truth is, after several weeks of seeing spectacular natural scenery all along our route, we found Butchart's formal gardens, featuring thousands and thousands of daffodils and multi-hued tulips, jarringly garish and artificial.

Such a narrow vision of what a garden should and should not be invites speculation: Would Pollan rewrite Genesis and refer instead to the weed-patch of Eden, for surely Jehovah did not employ a landscape designer?

Pollan also seems quite disturbed by what he calls the "environmental pretensions" of natural gardeners. I'm not exactly sure what he means by this odd phrase; is he suggesting dishonesty or self-delusion on their parts, as if, say, a store clerk were passing himself off as a brain surgeon? Surely, we should all be environmentalists in spirit as well as action. He, at least, refrained from referring to us as "environmental whackos" and "treehuggers," favorite epithets of the Rush Limbaugh crowd.

In fact, pretentious is the last word that would occur to me in describing the nativists I know. Level-headed, sensitive, and caring are more appropriate adjectives. It's open season on environmentalists these days, not just in magazine articles and talk shows, but over a beer at Joe's Tavern and around the dinner table as well. And the reason isn't hard to figure out: If what environmentalists are saying is true about the sorry state of our planet—if it's only partially true—then that's scary as Hell. It's much easier to ridicule than to change. Denial can be very comforting.

If, as Pollan states, going native and natural puts a moral burden on gardeners—giving up all those chemicals and all that over-watering—then so be it. And high time, too.

A more recent example of antinative propaganda appeared in the August 21, 1998, issue of the *Wall Street Journal.* In an article titled "Where the Wild Things Are," the author, Rebecca Lowell, told readers that having a natural landscape would place family members in harm's way. And to back up her thesis, she interviewed homeowners with "naturescapes" from around the country.

Anyone the least bit knowledgeable about the subject saw at once how biased and erroneous this article was. But most readers probably took it at face value and, as a result, ranked the idea of having a natural landscape just below having a tax audit on their list of favorite things to do. After all, this article was in the *Wall Street Journal*!

When I first read the article I assumed that Lowell had found and quoted people who agreed with her premise. Imagine my surprise when I tracked down most of the people cited—in fact, I already knew several of them—and got a very different slant on the story.

In the article, Coleen Kremer of St. Petersburg, Florida, was quoted on the subject of black snakes, which, according to Lowell, lurk in the Kremers's tall grass and threaten life and limb. "The snakes sneak up on me, then I jump and scream," Coleen said in the article. "Nonsense," said her husband, Jeff, when we talked on the phone a few weeks after the article came out. "Coleen was totally misquoted. Black snakes are very common around here, no matter what kind of landscape you have. They're harmless and nobody takes them seriously."

The Kremers were also, according to the *WSJ* article, responsible for their neighborhood being bombarded by yellow-crowned herons dropping "nasty bits of half-digested seafood" all over patios and deck furniture. One neighbor, Debra Bittner, was quoted as putting the blame squarely on the Kremers's natural landscape for this "scourge of pukeballs."

In fact, Mrs. Bittner told me that the tone of her comments had been totally skewed. "The article made me sound angry," she said. "I wasn't and I'm not. Anyway, it's not the Kremers's landscape that causes this. The herons have always lived in the tall pines we have around here, and I told that reporter that I'd rather live with the pukeballs than not have the herons."

"The thing that really upset us," Jeff told me, "aside from misquoting us—is that this reporter had an agenda. She deliberately misrepresented to us what the story was going to be about. We thought she was writing a positive piece."

The word agenda popped up in some of my other follow-up interviews. Greg Rubin, a San Diego landscape designer, and the only professional cited by Lowell, was very outspoken about the article. "It was totally bogus and out of line," he told me. "Rebecca Lowell admitted to me that she knew nothing about gardening, and it shows. She interviewed me and two of my clients at great length, and then picked a few comments out of context to make *her* point."

When I attempted to talk to one of Greg's clients, the man's wife said he wouldn't talk to me or any other writer—he was that angry about how his statements had been misrepresented.

Joy Buslaff, an artist in Big Bend, Wisconsin, was another of the misquoted interviewees. The natural pond that she'd put in was presented as being a magnet for "thousands of toads" that overran her property. In fact, Joy told me, there were only three toads. Later, she did have thousands of tadpoles, but "nature being what it is, almost all of them disappeared, eaten by other creatures. "Frankly," Joy said, "I have more problems with the neighbors' dogs than I do with wildlife."

No doubt the scariest part of Lowell's article for many was reading that Colorado residents Mark and Sarah Squire had predatory coyotes in their children's sandbox. The Squires's home, which is situated in the foothills of Cheyenne Mountain high above Colorado Springs, is in an area where such wildlife is often seen. The animals are a natural part of the environment and are frequently spotted in the landscapes of all the neighbors, *even those who have conventional lawn-centered landscapes.*

In the article, Sarah was quoted as saying, "if a coyote can take down a cow, it can certainly take down my three-year-old daughter!" But, according to Brooks Sahy, executive director of the Predator Defense Institute in Eugene, Oregon, "No coyote—or even a pair of them—could take down a cow. Ninety percent of a coyote's diet is rodents." The vast majority of such concerns, he adds, have more to do with what people imagine might happen, not what could or would really happen.

Sarah Squires says that she too was misquoted. "I never said that about the cow," she protested. "We see coyotes all the time, but we're certainly not scared of them. Once, we even saw a bear perched in a neighbor's tree."

Neighbor Carrie Trookman reflected the comments of the other area residents I talked to about the wildlife situation. "We certainly don't live in fear of them. We're more likely to reach for a camera than a gun," she said. "After all, we moved into their neighborhood, they didn't move into ours."

The tragedy is that many of these articles get reprinted all over the country, spreading the distortions and nonsense. The *WSJ* piece, for example, was reprinted in the *Chicago Tribune* and the *Fort Worth Star-Telegram*, as well as a number of other newspapers. And because it's in black-and-white, people tend to believe it.

P.S.: After I'd completed my follow-up interviews, I offered the evidence to Lowell's editors at *WSJ*. They were not interested in printing a retraction.

CHAPTER

47

To Save the Planet,
Save the Plants

Sally

Y ou've seen the bumper stickers: *Save the Whales. Save the Tigers. Save the Elephants.* It's scary how we're gradually—and in some cases, not so gradually—eliminating entire species of animals.

The case made by naturalists over and over again states that each one of these creatures is an important piece in the vast mosaic of life on our home planet. We are all interdependent. If we lose one species, it affects us all, perhaps in ways that we do not yet understand or appreciate.

As an animal lover I am, of course, concerned. But, as a passionate plant lover, I can't help but notice that an important part of the save-the-animals story is not being told effectively—specifically, that we *can*not save these animals unless we also save their habitats. We can eliminate all of the ivory poaching, all of the whaling ships, all of the big game sports hunters . . . and we would still lose these creatures.

Don't animal naturalists realize that plants are part of that mosaic? Those wild animals didn't evolve in zoos, eating baled hay or vitamin-enhanced cat food, and lounging under plastic awnings for shelter. They grazed on prairies, browsed shrubs, and hunted herbivores. And they mated, rested, and nested in thickets, forests, prairies, and marshes—vegetational environments.

It is not enough that we recognize that individual animal species are threatened; we must appreciate the relationships that exist among *all* species, both animal and plant. They overlap and intertwine in ever-widening circles to ultimately encompass the whole earth.

Plant life supports animal life, but it works the other way, too; insects fertilize the flowers, and birds and mammals distribute the seeds that are not sown by the wind.

We're not talking about something that occurs only in distant and exotic lands. Here at home, wolves, bears, and other native American animals are at risk of becoming zoological has-beens. And that's because they are losing their native habitats. The wide-open spaces for wild trees and shrubs are dwindling. And with them the seeds, nuts, and fruits, and the insects, birds, and rodents—all of which are a part of the support system that keeps bigger animals alive.

Sometimes this strikes me as being so obvious that I feel self-conscious even going on like this. But then I look at how we are devastating *our* remnant native vegetation to support *African* refugee animals in wildlife parks.

And I wonder why we are clear-cutting our forests and replanting cash crops when selective cutting can provide timber and retain habitat. A plantation of pines is not a forest habitat. It is a sterile monoculture, without underbrush, berries, mushrooms, or varied native saplings growing up through the thick layers of pine needles. These tree plantations are unnaturally silent; the singing of birds is rarely heard here.

As we, as a nation, become more knowledgeable and environmentally sophisticated, we can support enlightened legislation and conservation efforts on a larger scale. We need vast tracts of land that are allowed to be wild. We don't have enough publicly owned lands, so we need to add private land. Owners of dozens of ranches and ranchettes have adopted conservation easements, but we need more, because we need to link the big tracts of land with corridors of wildland if we're to keep the larger predators alive.

Furthermore, we need new laws to protect these large tracts of land and their interlinking corridors for wildlife.

On government lands, we need to change the sixteenth-century laws that sell off grazing and timber cutting rights for a fraction of their real value. These laws were originally an offshoot of English commons law. The purpose was to let subsistence farmers graze their livestock on commonly held (i.e., public) summer pastures and save the home pasture for winter. They were to let homeowners cut firewood for cooking and heating and making furniture.

There are still a few small farmers in northern New Mexico who rely on summer pastures (and a job in town) to keep their family farms. But most of the grazing rights are used by the big cattle outfits, just as clear-cutting benefits rich investors far more than it does lumberjacks. As taxpayers we're getting a pittance for grazing and timber rights and we're subsidizing rich guys at the top who have monthly incomes greater than our annual incomes.

We also need new land laws that give the same tax break for conservation management that is given for agricultural use. That way, many millions of acres no longer needed for farming could be converted to conservation.

Besides the big picture, there is much we can do all on our own, and the most basic thing we can *all* do is to plant native trees, shrubs, flowers, and grasses in our home gardens.

Sure, I know. Just your garden won't keep mountain lions and herds of bison alive. But it can make a big difference for songbirds, butterflies, bees, and hawk moths. Then, imagine what could happen if all of your neighbors did the same thing. Instead of just your quarter-acre lot, the natural garden could encompass a twelve-acre block, even a fifty-acre neighborhood.

When natural landscapes are used on larger pieces of property that also adjoin creeks or ponds, they become habitats that can attract and support larger wildlife such as owls, hawks, raccoons, opossums, and foxes. These animals are not dangerous to humans; we have been dangerous to them Given the chance, they can live very peaceably in close proximity to us. Remember, good neighbors come in all species.

We need to save parcels out of development tracts—natural green spaces that can serve as havens for wildlife. We need to replant existing but barren parks. On these larger plots, we can preserve a much greater diversity of native plants than would be suitable for typical urban gardens. Wildflowers, rampant berry bushes, tangles, and thickets vital for nesting birds would flourish in these places. Here, too, we could leave rotting logs that are vital to the life cycles of far more creatures than we realize.

It's easier to be heard by your county or city officials if you belong to an organization. Most states have native plant societies, wildflower clubs, or prairie associations. These groups dispense information, hold field trips and lectures, plant gardens, and help maintain preserves.

On the national level, there are Wild Ones Natural Landscapers, Sierra Club, and The Nature Conservancy. In the first edition, we suggested you contact the clearinghouse at the Lady Bird Johnson Wildflower Center, 4801 LaCrosse Blvd., Austin, TX 78739, or call them at 512-292-4200. This will still work, but so will a simple Internet search. Most of the above-mentioned organizations are linked to open to you a whole world of conservation and native plant gardening.

Truth or Consequences

Sally

A friend of mine, Neil Diboll of Prairie Nursery in Wisconsin, recently said: "In nature there is no right or wrong; there are only consequences." I think this is true. Even a casual observation of our landscapes shows that Mother Nature has no prejudice against alien and invasive plants. Nature abhors a vacuum, and she doesn't care which species of plants hold the soil as long as something—*anything*—does.

Much of our efforts at restoring and reconstructing native landscapes are based on our earliest data, when North American vegetation was least influenced by European imports and land management. This, necessarily, means that our concepts of what is truly native reflect which plants were recorded by botanists in the early days of settlement and exploration. The bulk of our information comes from the work of Asa Gray, professor of botany at Harvard University, who received pressed plants from explorers all over what is now the United States and published his first manual in 1848.

The first scientific observations made west of the Mississippi River were in 1803 by the Lewis and Clark Expedition. When they explored the sources of the Missouri River, crossed the Rockies, and wintered near the mouth of the Columbia River in the Pacific Northwest, the land they were traversing was uncharacteristically lush and overgrown. This was so for two reasons. The impact of Native American populations on the land had recently been reduced by more than half because of widespread and devastating epidemics of European diseases. And the climate had been unusually cool and moist since 1600. Known as the Little Ice Age, this cooling trend ended in 1850, just as Americans of European descent populated western North America and plowed up the prairies.

Since then, the climate has been, on the average, warming. So, although we are basing our knowledge of native plants on where they were about 1850, we are dealing with warmer and drier conditions. Warmer temperatures mean less moisture because of evaporation. If rainfall doesn't increase with rising temperatures, drought occurs.

Droughts are serious because we don't have the technology to remedy them. In Taos, New Mexico, where Andy and I now live, wells are going dry, and rivers and lakes are half full. Forest fires have become frequent, and they are not the beneficial ground or surface fires that occurred every decade in prehistoric times. The trees contain less moisture than ordinary lumber and they are jammed close together. The result is that any lightning strike or carelessly managed campfire can cause a devastating crown fire.

If the drought continues, there will be a permanent shift in vegetation here. Big sagebrush, the cornerstone of an ecosystem called Basin and Range that extends up into Canada, is beginning to die here in its southernmost toe, and if it does, the soft bluegreen vistas Taos is famous for will be replaced by brown blowing topsoil.

I think that what we are talking about here are visible signs of global warming. This is a controversial topic, fraught with politics, but it cannot be denied that our world is getting warmer. Glacier Park in Montana had 150 glaciers when it was mapped in the late 1800s, and now it has only 35. The famous "snows" of Kilimanjaro in Africa lost more than 80 percent of their area in the 1900s. The Qori Kalis glacier in the Andes is shrinking at a rate of nearly two feet a day. The sea ice that covers the North Pole is thinning, and in Antarctica huge sections of the Larsen B ice shelf collapsed in 1995 and 2002, letting at least five glaciers loose to start slipping toward the ocean. When they arrive, sea levels will rise.

Climates all over the globe are changing before our eyes. In the past, there has been sufficient time for forests to retreat northward or to higher elevations where temperatures are cooler and evaporation less fierce. There has been sufficient time for new species to evolve as the deserts expanded. In this century, the plants will need our help.

What I've observed is that southwestern grasslands established before 1850 can hang on in severe drought, going dormant when conditions are especially tough and coming to life whenever rains allow. But that once those grasslands are destroyed, they do not regenerate on their own. They are gone forever unless we replant them, and in the Southwest they need to be irrigated to germinate and irrigated again to grow enough to form a soil-holding cover. The result? Nonnatives adapted to harsh climates, disturbed soil, and human intervention are taking over.

But even in eastern forests and Midwestern prairies, where rainfall is sufficient for germination of native species without supplemental irrigation, alien invasive plants are taking over. Our native plants support a complex web of mammals, birds, and insects, and because plant roots prevent soil erosion, they are also vital to clean water, fish, and amphibians. If our continent becomes populated only by nonnative invasive species, our lives will be greatly impoverished.

So, we're facing two problems if we wish to maintain our rich botanical heritage here in North America—a warming climate and invasive species.

Where we can create wildlife corridors, wild species will be able to move around as the climate changes. Where we can't, we may have to start replanting our native lands.

This sounds daunting, but we have been subsidizing ranchers and farmers to do this for decades. The focus has been on the health of cattle and other livestock, and the seed has been alfalfa and nonnative grasses. But we could change that. We could grow, harvest, market, and plant native seeds.

Where the land is essentially undisturbed, this would not be necessary, because the more drought-tolerant species are already built into the native diversity. But we have little intact land left. American Indians maintained rich and healthy ecosystems, and we of European heritage have almost completely destroyed our native landed wealth.

Ecologists are developing techniques for restoring and re-creating prairies, savannas, and forests, but the efforts I've seen are to restore the ecosystems that existed in 1850 or 1700 or whenever American Indians were last in charge. We need these skills, and these are definitely the best guidelines we have.

But maybe we need to change the focus to figure out which new configurations of American plants are most likely to succeed in our changing climate. In Taos, for example, I would choose to plant those grasses native to us that are also native to hotter drier places nearby like Albuquerque and Farmington. Those grasses should have the best chance of being able to germinate with our new heat and reduced rainfall. And I don't mean choose one grass to plant. I mean choose ten grasses and twenty flowers to plant, so that each ecological niche can be filled.

As to the alien invasive species, I don't think we can just pour poisons on those we don't like, either because they are not native to the Americas or because cattle don't like to eat them. Poisons hurt far more organisms than the plants we target. Plus, it is not likely that we will completely remove these plants from our continent. They are here to stay, whether we like it or not.

Without our interference, most of these invasives would probably be quickly absorbed into the existing landscapes. Russian olive and tamarisk or privet and Japanese honeysuckle would be coexisting with, not crowding out, our native cottonwood bottomlands if we hadn't built dams to stop annual flooding on our rivers. Invasives would not be overrunning our eastern forests if we installed power lines without bulldozing the ground underneath them with bulldozer blades contaminated with weed seeds. Our roadsides could as easily be revegetated with natives as alien invasives, and many highway departments are working hard on this.

Maybe it's because I'm more of a positive person than a negative one, but I think that the answer is not to poison what we don't want, but to plant what we do want—not to destroy, but to maintain for what we want. If we mow regularly, we get some semblance of a lawn. If we mow once a year, we get a prairie. If we burn once a decade, we get a savanna. If we burn once a century, we get a forest.

We humans live all over the world. We shape all landscapes. Native Americans managed the landscapes of North America for maximum health, and they did a good job. I bet modern Americans are smart enough to do it too. We just need to make it a priority. We need to think long term instead of short term. We need to be generous instead of greedy. Then we all benefit.

We haven't the time to take our time.

—EUGENE IONESCO

Although we've covered a lot of ground in these pages, we feel as if we've barely scratched the surface. Hardly a day goes by when we don't learn something new and exciting about native plants—usually from observing them in the wild, often from lay gardeners like you who were just messing around in their own gardens and learned what a certain plant will or won't do.

Native plant landscaping is going to have as profoundly positive an effect on our gardens and our environment as our new and enlightened ideas on nutrition are having on our health. Using native plants is far more than just another way to make your garden look pretty—it actually has the potential to change the world for the better. And how many things can you say that about these days?

About the Authors

Sally Wasowski is a nationally respected landscape designer and author. She has written for publications such as *Texas Gardener*, *Northern Gardener*, and a number of Brooklyn Botanic Garden handbooks. For seven years Sally taught sold-out classes on landscape design at Southern Methodist University's School of Continuing Education, and was a founding member and past president of the Texas Native Plant Society. She is currently publications chair for the Native Plant Society of New Mexico.

Andy Wasowski is a freelance writer and photographer specializing in gardening and environmental issues. He has written for magazines such as *Sierra*, *Fine Gardening*, *Audubon*, and *The American Gardener*. In addition, he has done on-air commentaries for National Public Radio's *Living on Earth*. Andy is the newsletter editor for the Native Plant Society of New Mexico.

Sally and Andy are regional editors for *Wildflower* magazine, honorary directors of the Wild Ones, and have been honored for their work by the Canadian Wildflower Society and the American Horticultural Society. They live in northern New Mexico with their cats, Felix and Fanny. Their website is www.botanicalmissionaries.com.

Vahan Shirvanian's cartoons have appeared in the *Saturday Evening Post*, *Playboy*, *New Yorker*, *Boys Life*, and dozens of other national and regional publications.